› **FLAVOURS OF VANCOUVER**

Compiled by SHEILA PEACOCK and JOAN CROSS

FLAVOURS *of* VANCOUVER

DISHES FROM AROUND THE WORLD

DOUGLAS & McINTYRE

Vancouver/Toronto

Dedicated to my Dad ... thank you for always believing there's nothing I can't do.
LOVE, SHEILA

Thanks to my mother, Clara Hill, who always allowed me access to her kitchen, and my husband, Sid, my soul mate in our passionate pursuit of food and wine.
JOAN CROSS

Douglas & McIntyre
2323 Quebec Street, Suite 201
Vancouver, British Columbia
Canada V5T 4S7
www.douglas-mcintyre.com

Library and Archives Canada Cataloguing in Publication
Peacock, Sheila, 1964–
Flavours of Vancouver : dishes from around the world / compiled by Sheila Peacock and Joan Cross.
Includes index.
ISBN-13: 978-1-55365-148-2 · ISBN-10: 1-55365-148-0
1. Cookery. I. Cross, Joan, 1939– II. Title.
TX725.P42 2005   641.5   C2005-905282-1

Editing by Elizabeth Wilson
Cover and text design by Jessica Sullivan
Cover photo by Jessica Sullivan
Printed and bound in Canada by Friesens
Printed on acid-free paper that is forest friendly (100% post-consumer recycled paper) and has been processed chlorine free.

We gratefully acknowledge the financial support of the Canada Council for the Arts, the British Columbia Arts Council, and the Government of Canada through the Book Publishing Industry Development Program (BPIDP) for our publishing activities.

Partial proceeds from the sale of this book are going to Save the Children Canada, to help children around the world. Save the Children Canada has been working for more than eighty years, both in Canada and overseas, to bring immediate and lasting improvements to children's lives through the realization of their rights. Save the Children Canada works under the broad categories of HIV/AIDS, exploitation and abuse, conflict and disaster, and education. Save the Children Canada is a non-political, non-religious organization committed to long-term development at the grassroots level through partnerships with local communities, government bodies and international organizations. Save the Children Canada is a member of the International Save the Children Alliance. For more information, check out their Web site at www.savethechildren.ca.

CONTENTS

MAIN DISHES

Sharing food stories and recipes means sharing a bit of yourself with friends new and old. In Vancouver, it also means globetrotting without leaving your neighbourhood café, or even your own kitchen. There are so many international flavours to choose from, and so many fabulous cooks to learn from, that even everyday food discoveries are a cause for celebration—and talk!

Flavours of Vancouver celebrates the bountiful culinary skills and memorable stories of CBC Radio friends who call Vancouver, and Canada, home. Some recipes come from families who have been here for generations; others are from new Canadians who are bringing their traditions to Vancouver tables. There are even some that were discovered on global adventures and brought home to share. Most of the recipes are from home kitchens, but we've sprinkled in some from Vancouver's finest chefs, along with their personal stories. People whose voices you hear on CBC Radio also contributed their culinary talents to this collection. With each recipe is a story that illustrates, yet again, why food and conversation go together.

From the CBC Radio kitchen table to yours, we hope you enjoy this collection of recipes celebrating the flavours, and people, of Vancouver.

Sheila Peacock
CBC Radio Specials Producer

⌐ ACKNOWLEDGEMENTS

The recipes in this collection were tested by Joan Cross, who has studied with some of the best chefs and teachers in the world—and even *she* learned about ingredients and techniques she hadn't tried before. Thank you, Joan, for being such an enthusiastic, dedicated and thorough culinary detective! I would also like to thank Andy Lung for his help with translations and extra investigations—we now know what "plaster" powder is! Also, a big thank you to CBC Radio's Theresa Lalonde for her two-week series profiling adult ESL teachers and students throughout the Lower Mainland, and for her help in bringing their stories and recipes to this cookbook. The final manuscript was beautifully edited and painstakingly checked by Elizabeth Wilson, who wields her red pen with remarkable patience and good humour—thank you, Ibby.

VERY SPECIAL THANKS TO:

The fabulous hosts and producers of CBC Radio's *The Early Edition, B.C. Almanac, On the Coast* and *North by Northwest*

Everyone at Douglas & McIntyre, especially Rob Sanders, Susan Rana, Liza Algar and Pam Robertson

Vancouver Community College

The Canadian Immigrant Magazine

Fairchild Radio

CCM of Canada

> # LIGHT DISHES, SNACKS

and CONDIMENTS

DUTCH PANCAKE

DARLENE EATON

Sick of bacon and eggs or French toast for break-fast? Where would we be without the mouth-watering, unique flavour of the world-famous Dutch pancake? My grandmother, Anna Iverson, was from Norway but her specialties were Swedish meatballs for dinner and the Dutch pancake for week-end breakfast.

1 tsp butter, melted
2 large eggs
½ cup all-purpose flour
½ cup skim milk
1 Tbsp granulated sugar
pinch of nutmeg
½ fresh lemon
1 tsp icing sugar

> SERVES 3–4

PREHEAT the oven to 350°F. Swirl melted butter in a 10-inch shallow glass pie plate, spreading it from side to side. In a separate bowl, thoroughly mix eggs, flour, milk and granulated sugar with a whisk or beater, and then mix in the pinch of nutmeg. Pour the batter into the pie plate and place in the oven. Bake for about 15 minutes, until the pancake rises gently and turns a golden-cream colour. Remove from the oven, and squeeze fresh lemon juice over the entire pancake while it's still warm. Then dust the entire surface with icing sugar. Cut into wedges and serve hot. You can also add fresh straw-berries or other seasonal fruit.

NOTE For a lighter texture, separate the egg and mix the yolk in with the flour, milk and granulated sugar. Beat the white separately to soft peaks and then fold it into the flour mixture.

› BING

RUTH CASEY AND DOUG FRIESEN

Several years ago we were in Beijing, on holiday with Doug's brother and his two young kids. Waking up our first morning in China, severely jet-lagged and quite disoriented, we set out from our small guesthouse to find some breakfast and explore the city. Along the city streets, we noticed several sidewalk carts selling some sort of pancake that people were eating like a sandwich. Eventually, in a park full of elderly tai chi practitioners, we succumbed to hunger and curiosity and approached one of the carts. Even the kids were eager to try something in this exotic land full of strange sights, smells and sounds. What we tried (and became quite addicted to) are known as *bing*. These delightful breakfast packages consist of freshly made, tender crêpes cooked with a layer of egg, brushed with hoisin and chili, garnished with fresh cilantro leaves and black sesame seeds, and folded into a convenient parcel for tidy eating.

We wolfed ours down almost as quickly as the women working the carts expertly made them. It was delightful sitting on a park bench on a cold November Beijing morning, eating hot, nutritious and intensely flavourful food, the steam rising from the bing into the cool morning air.

We went out for our bing fix each morning we were there, and set out to learn how to make them when we returned to Vancouver. Each bite takes us back to morning in Beijing. We've heard the city is changing dramatically, particularly in the build-up to the 2008 Olympics, and truly hope that the bing carts haven't all been lost in the rush for "development." If nothing else, we've managed to preserve the recipe and the memories, and keep them with us here in Vancouver.

CRÊPES
1 cup all-purpose flour
pinch of salt
1¼ cups milk
2 large eggs

TOPPING (PER CRÊPE)
1 egg
dash of salt
handful of cilantro leaves, washed and patted dry
1 tsp hoisin sauce
½ tsp sambal oelek (Indonesian chili paste), to taste
¼ tsp black sesame seeds (optional)

CRÊPES: Combine flour, salt and milk, beating until smooth. Beat in eggs. Allow batter to rest 1 hour in refrigerator, if possible, before cooking.

ASSEMBLY: Lightly butter a 10-inch non-stick frying pan and heat over medium heat. Stir the crêpe batter. Pour ⅓ cup crêpe batter into the pan and swirl to cover the bottom as thinly as possible (thin out with milk or water if it's too thick). When just cooked on one side, flip it. Crack egg on top, lightly scramble it and add salt. When the egg starts to solidify, flip the crêpe again (egg will be on the bottom). Brush the top of the crêpe lightly with hoisin sauce then sambal oelek, sprinkle cilantro over the crêpe, then finish with a sprinkling of black sesame seeds. The egg should be cooked by now. Make four light marks with lifter to form a square on the round crêpe, fold the rounded sides in, fold the whole thing in half, then in half again. The bing is now ready to eat! You can hold it in a paper towel, like you would a sandwich.

CHINESE PANCAKES

EVELYN TRAVIS

This recipe came from somewhere in Vietnam. I'm not too sure if that's where it originated, but that's where my mom is from. I would like to share this recipe to honour my grandmother and mother. My grandma passed away before I could ever meet her but she passed this recipe on to my mom. My mom, who was a refugee, managed to escape from Vietnam and make it to Canada. That's how I came to this world and I'm thankful that I'm here. This simple recipe is called Chinese Pancakes. We usually eat it on the weekend, when everyone's home. My roommate didn't like it at first but now she's the one who suggests we make it on Saturday mornings. Even my African Amazon parrot enjoys these pancakes!

2 cups all-purpose flour
warm water (about ⅔ cup)
4 Chinese sausages, rinsed and cut into ¼-inch pieces
6 green onions, washed and sliced
½ cup preserved radish, rinsed and chopped
1 Tbsp oil

MAKES ABOUT 12 PANCAKES

PLACE flour in a large bowl and gradually stir in warm water. (It must be warm water or else the dough will end up tasting funny. Believe me, I know.) Add just enough water to hold the mixture together. Knead very gently until you have a nice soft dough. Turn the dough out onto a floured surface.

MIX sausages, green onions and radish in a medium-sized bowl.

TAKE a small handful of dough into your hand and flatten it in your palm. Take a spoonful of the sausage mixture and place it in the centre of the dough. Do not overfill. Seal the dough around the filling by pinching the edges together to form a ball. Place it on a floured plate and repeat with the rest of the dough and filling. Make sure the balls don't stick together or to the plate.

HEAT oil in a large frying pan over medium heat. Place the balls in the pan one at a time, pressing down on each with a spatula. Continue until the pan is full of nice flattened Chinese pancakes. Once the first side is golden brown, reduce the heat and flip the pancakes. Press down and let them sizzle. Cooking time is about 3 to 4 minutes per side depending upon the thickness of the dough and the heat used. Repeat until all the pancakes are done. Serve immediately.

I LIKE to eat these pancakes with a honey garlic sauce but you can try any sauce you like.

WHAMPAO SCRAMBLED EGGS

TONY LUK

My hometown is a small village in the Whampao District of Guangzhou in China. When I was small, my uncle told me how the national father of the Chinese republic, Dr. Sun Yat-sen, and Mr. Chiang Kai-shek, the commandant of the Whampao Military Academy, enjoyed a dish in a small restaurant near our village. Though it was only a simple scrambled egg dish, it was so appreciated by these two famous politicians that the name of the dish is Whampao Scrambled Eggs, to commemorate them. When I immigrated to Vancouver, I taught this quick and easy dish to my daughter, hoping that she and her future children will remember her hometown in China.

1 cup chives
2 Tbsp vegetable oil
1 tsp salt
2 Tbsp water
6 large eggs, beaten

> SERVES 4–6

WASH, drain, dry and cut the chives into ½-inch pieces. (Kitchen scissors work well.) Pour oil into a preheated frying pan over medium heat. Add chives and cook for about 1 minute. Add salt. Add water to eggs, mix with a fork and pour the egg mixture into the frying pan. Scramble lightly and let sit for a minute until eggs are solidified to your taste.

› MOM'S MARVELLOUS PRAWNS

KENNETH CHOOI

My mother's prawn dish originated in Malaysia, where fusion cooking was being enjoyed long before its popularity now. It was taught to her by her mother, and I have learned to make it by watching and preparing it with her. My mother told me that cars passing the kitchen window would slow down because of the beautiful scent of this dish. A combination of Indian spices, Chinese cooking techniques and Western adaptation, it can be cooked in a short period of time and is healthy and delicious! Vancouver's superb selection of local seafood always makes this dish an easy one. I have prepared these prawns as a formal entrée, for potluck dinners and as a snack. The dish's flexibility is endless and it always tastes just as good or better the next day.

2–3 Tbsp vegetable oil
1 medium onion, chopped
2 cloves garlic, chopped
½ tsp turmeric
1 tsp ground cumin
1 tsp garam masala
¾ lb uncooked peeled prawns
2 Tbsp plain yogurt
1 Tbsp chopped cilantro
   or parsley
salt, to taste
lemon wedges for garnish
   (optional)

› SERVES 4

HEAT OIL in a frying pan or wok over medium-high heat and fry onion and garlic for 30 seconds, stirring. Add turmeric, cumin and garam masala and stir-fry for 2 minutes. Add prawns and cook until they turn pink. Add yogurt and cilantro or parsley, then salt to taste. Stir-fry for another 2 minutes, until prawns become opaque. Mix thoroughly and serve.

SERVE the prawns with crusty French bread or on a bed of rice. Garnish with lemon wedges. Perfect with a small salad and any type of wine—my favourite is a nice Shiraz!

SHIITAKE MUSHROOM–CRUSTED SCALLOPS
WITH GINGER SCALLION PISTOU

CAROL CHOW, *Hart House Restaurant*

I'm third-generation Chinese-Canadian. My dad was born here and my mom was born in China. Appreciating good food is something that's ingrained in me because food and family go together in Chinese culture. Both of my parents love to cook, but Dad's repertoire includes both Western and Chinese dishes, while Mom strictly cooks Chinese. Growing up, I followed the more traditional route of going to business school, but I hated it, so when my mom asked me what I would really like to do, and I said I wanted to be a chef, my parents were very supportive. I went to the prestigious Dubrulle Culinary Institute, and then worked for some of the best restaurateurs in the city, including John Bishop and Umberto Menghi. When I became Executive Chef of Hart House Restaurant on Deer Lake, I moved the menu to more of a seafood theme. This recipe reflects my love of local ingredients combined with tastes from my childhood.

GINGER SCALLION PISTOU
4 cups water
1 bunch scallions, washed and sliced
bowl of ice water
1 cup peeled fresh ginger, sliced
½ cup olive oil
pinch of salt

SCALLOPS
16 large scallops
2 tsp vegetable oil
½ cup dried shiitake mushrooms, ground
sea salt
pepper

> SERVES 4

GINGER SCALLION PISTOU: Bring water to a boil and immerse scallions for a few seconds. Remove scallions and place in ice water to stop the cooking process. Remove from ice water, drain well and set aside. Purée ginger with oil and salt. Place the mixture in a small pot or pan and heat to warm. Remove from heat and let cool. Combine scallions and ginger in a blender and process until smooth. Place in a squeeze bottle or small container. Refrigerate until ready to use. It will keep for at least 1 week.

SCALLOPS: Place scallops on a paper towel. Heat a frying pan over high heat and add vegetable oil to coat the bottom for searing. Dip scallops into shiitake dust and then put in the hot pan. Sear well and turn over. Cook 30 more seconds and place on a plate. Season with salt and pepper. Drizzle Ginger Scallion Pistou over scallops.

SERVE with sticky rice, fried rice or Asian noodles.

› CLAM FRITTERS

DOLLY WATTS, *Liliget Feast House*

I am Git'ksan from the house of Ghu'sen, at Gitsegukela, B.C. My mother, Chief Mel'hus, late Martha Morgan, married Chief Axtl-hix Gibu, late Wallace Morgan, from Gitwangk (also known as Kitwanga) village. I'm the tenth of fourteen children, and we lived on the mighty Skeena River. It was our food basket, supporting a beautiful variety of animals, fish, birds, berries and vegetables. I grew up in a time of change and turmoil, forced to leave my family to live in residential schools, but all of my experiences inspired me to work hard and be entrepreneurial. I first set up Just Like Grandma's Bannock Catering in 1992, and in 1995 opened the Liliget Feast House, where we serve a bounty of First Nations foods. This is a favourite recipe from our restaurant, with Liliget's own sweet and sour sauce for a dip.

› MAKES 12 SMALL FRITTERS

LILIGET SWEET AND SOUR SAUCE: Mix brown sugar and cornstarch in a saucepan. Stir in the rest of the ingredients. Heat and stir until the sauce boils and thickens. Set aside.

CLAM FRITTERS: Mix all ingredients, except egg whites, in a bowl or food processor. The resulting batter will be a bit lumpy. In a separate bowl, beat egg whites until they form soft peaks. Fold into the batter. In a deep pot, heat oil to 350°F. Use a small scoop or a tablespoon to drop portions of the batter into the pot. Fry until light brown, turning once. Cook a few at a time, without crowding them. Remove with a slotted spoon and place on a paper-towel-lined tray to blot any excess oil. Serve with Liliget Sweet and Sour Sauce.

LILIGET SWEET AND SOUR SAUCE
- 2 cups brown sugar
- 4 tsp cornstarch
- 2 Tbsp soy sauce
- ½ cup water
- ½ cup white vinegar
- 1 Tbsp ketchup

CLAM FRITTERS
- 1¼ cups all-purpose flour
- ¼ tsp baking powder
- ¼ tsp lemon pepper
- ¼ medium onion, diced
- 1 stalk celery, diced
- ½ of a 284-mL can of baby clams with nectar
- ¼ cup egg whites (about 1 large egg white)
- vegetable oil (enough to come to a depth of 2 inches in the pot)

CEVICHE PIURANO

CHRISTINE LAZARTE

At one time, my entire knowledge of Peru was limited to the recollection of a few *National Geographic* photos of beautifully dressed Andean people weaving vibrant colours on lush mountainsides. Then I arrived in Peru to work for eight months. Out of Lima's concrete streets rose haphazard brick buildings, rebar from unfinished construction jutting into the grey sky. I then went to the north of the country, to Piura, a small city coaxed from the barren coastal desert. Uneven sidewalks bordered broken concrete streets covered in blowing sand and garbage. Houses were only partially visible behind brick walls topped with spikes or glass shards. Soon after arriving we drove in the sweltering mid-morning heat through the noisy downtown, along the highway until it turned into hard-packed sand. At times the smell of sewage blew over us with the sand and dust from the road. We were at the edge of town, where the tiny houses were built from mud and straw mats. I'm certain that water, heat and sewer services were severely limited. In this desolate neighbourhood we saw a young woman with a neatly ironed knee-length skirt and matching blouse, shined shoes and luscious hair that framed her carefully made-up face. How did she accomplish such beauty when I, with my gringo dollars and hot showers, have never approximated such loveliness? In this area was the best restaurant in the city for ceviche. We sat in a shaded veranda, our table was covered with a crisp tablecloth, and the waiters were dressed like they worked in a fine hotel. Our meal was raw seafood that had been soaked in a lime juice marinade and was served with thinly sliced onions. In Peru, ceviche is usually enjoyed before noon so that the fish is fresh from the morning catch. Saturday and Sunday mornings are the best times to eat ceviche because it will cure the hangover from the night before. I had expected something like sushi, but this was different. The acid of the lime opened my taste buds so they could welcome the heat of the chilies and the subtle flavours of the fish.

2 lb raw, boneless, white-fleshed fish (such as halibut)
juice of 10 limes (try to find tart, juicy, flavourful Peruvian or Mexican limes)
salt (about 1 tsp)
1 hot banana pepper (use a small jalapeño if you prefer mild spiciness, or a combination of several hot chilies if you have an able tongue), seeded and very finely chopped
1 large red onion, very thinly sliced

16

I now have the opportunity to eat endless meals of ceviche, after marrying a Peruvian and bringing him and his recipes home. I may someday be able to make ceviche as well as my Peruvian family, but I doubt I will ever learn the Peruvian ability to create something beautiful from practically nothing. Many recipes for ceviche are very fancy, which I think hinders the dance of flavours in the simple ceviche recipes from Piura, Peru, boasted as the best place in the world to eat ceviche.

› SERVES 10–12

NOTE The fish used for ceviche must be extremely fresh and handled with the utmost concern for food safety. Keep the fish as cold as possible and clean and sanitize the work surfaces and knives thoroughly before and after use.

CUT FISH lengthwise into 1-inch strips using a sharp, non-serrated knife. Cut the strips into ½-inch lengths. Cover the bottom of a large, shallow non-metal (glass is ideal) casserole dish with some of the lime juice. Neatly arrange the fish pieces (no more than 2 pieces in depth) in the dish and sprinkle liberally with salt. Cover with lime juice. Add hot peppers to the dish. Carefully use a non-metal spoon to ensure that peppers are adequately distributed. Spread onion on top of the fish, ensuring it is well bathed in the lime juice. Add more lime juice if necessary. Cover.

MARINATE in the refrigerator for 3 to 4 hours. The length of time will depend largely on the acidity of the limes. The ceviche is ready when the flesh of the fish is opaque white (not transparent or pink) and appears cooked throughout.

DRAIN the ceviche and serve on a bed of lettuce with side dishes of yam, corn or other starchy vegetables.

NOBUE PEACOCK'S SQUARE OSHI SUSHI

SHEILA PEACOCK

I'm a somewhat rare breed in this city—a third-generation Vancouverite. My family roots extend back to England, Scotland, Ireland and Sweden and now we have new roots from Japan. My sister-in-law, Nobue, was born in Odawara, Kanagawa, Japan. She's a fantastic cook and we share a love not only of good food but also of healthy new recipes. This appetizer is her creation, bringing together traditional sushi skills from Japan with our fabulous wild West Coast smoked salmon. It's always a big hit with family and friends at parties—Nobue's famous for it!

> MAKES 20–25 PIECES

SUSHI RICE: Put rice in a large bowl. Fill the bowl with fresh water. Press rice 20 to 30 times with the heel of your hand. Pour off the opaque water. Repeat this procedure 3 or 4 times, until the water remains almost clear. Drain rice and let rest 30 minutes before cooking.

COMBINE rice vinegar, sugar and salt in a small pot and heat until sugar and salt dissolve. Remove from heat and set aside.

PLACE rice in a rice cooker (for best results). Add fresh water, about 2 cups, to just cover the rice. Put konbu on top, if using, and turn on the rice cooker.

When rice is cooked, transfer it to a wooden sushi bowl, or regular wooden bowl, moistened with water. Sprinkle the vinegar dressing all over the rice. Using a flat wooden spoon, toss the rice with horizontal, cutting strokes while fanning it with a hand fan in your other hand—this is the traditional method for mixing and cooling sushi rice. After rice is thoroughly mixed and cool to the touch, cover with a clean, wet cloth to keep it moist.

ASSEMBLY: This works best in a square metal baking pan with a removable bottom, but they're hard to find, so you can use any

SUSHI RICE
2 cups sushi rice
4 Tbsp rice vinegar
3 Tbsp + 1½ tsp granulated
  sugar
½ tsp salt
water (about 2 cups)
4-inch strip of konbu (kelp),
  optional

ASSEMBLY
1 nori seaweed sheet
  (8 × 8 inches)
8–10 thin slices B.C.
  smoked salmon
⅛ cup white sesame seeds,
  toasted

8-inch square dish—just line it with wax paper, up to the edges, so you can take the cut sushi pieces out without them falling apart.

NOTE Keep your hands wet throughout this procedure to keep the rice from sticking to your fingers!

PREPARE the dish by wiping it with a clean wet cloth (again, to prevent a sticky situation!). Spread the sushi rice in the pan, about ¾ of an inch thick. Press it down evenly with your wet hands. Put the nori sheet on top. Arrange the smoked salmon on top of the nori. Spread another ¾ of an inch of rice evenly on top of the smoked salmon. Sprinkle the rice with toasted sesame seeds. Wet your hands and gently but firmly press down on the sushi one more time. Cover the dish and refrigerate for at least 1 hour.

TO SERVE, cut the sushi into 1-inch squares. (Wipe the knife with a moistened cloth between cuts to make clean slices.) Serve with Japanese pickled ginger, wasabi paste and Japanese soy sauce.

BIS MORENO SCAMPI "SUSCI"

MORENO MIOTTO, *Bis Moreno Restaurant*

On a trip to trace my mother's roots in central Italy, on the Adriatic Sea, I was expecting to find lots of simple, inexpensive, grilled seafood because it's a kind of tourist area for Italians, who want cheap food on tour. But to my surprise I found a Michelin one-star restaurant where the chef, an Italian who trained in Japan, was trying to bring a greater appreciation for raw fish to Italians. The chef has even trademarked the spelling "susci" in Italy! This recipe was inspired by his Italian way of playing with fresh, raw seafood. Enjoy!

› SERVES 4

PREHEAT the oven to 375°F. Cut 3 of the tomatoes in half lengthwise and place skin-side down on a baking sheet. Season with sage, rosemary and oregano. Salt and pepper lightly and drizzle with oil. Roast until very soft and well done. Let tomatoes cool, then place in a small bowl. Mix with a spoon to a salsa consistency and add more salt and pepper if needed. Meanwhile, cut the remaining 3 tomatoes in half lengthwise and seed them. Cut into very small pieces and place in a bowl. Chiffonade basil by stacking leaves on top of each other and cutting into very thin strips crosswise. Add basil, garlic, salt, pepper and oil to tomatoes. This part of the recipe is best if made 2 hours before serving.

NOTE The prawns used for "susci" must be extremely fresh and handled with the utmost concern for food safety. Keep the prawns as cold as possible, and clean and sanitize the work surfaces and utensils thoroughly before and after use.

PLACE spot prawns in a small stainless-steel bowl. Add orange juice and drizzle oil into bowl. For the marinade to be acidic enough, ensure 4 parts orange juice to 1 part olive oil. Add a pinch of salt,

Preparation for two ingredients done two ways, raw and cooked, interacting with each other.

6 roma tomatoes, divided
2 fresh sage leaves, chopped
¼ tsp chopped fresh rosemary
pinch of dried oregano
salt and pepper
extra virgin olive oil
6 basil leaves
1 clove garlic, finely chopped
4 B.C. spot prawns, peeled
juice of 1 large orange
4 Icelandic scampi tails or
   the largest tiger prawns
   you can find

making sure all prawns are salted, and let stand approximately
10 to 12 minutes to marinate and slightly cure.

BUTTERFLY scampi (cut down centre back and open up), making sure
they are clean and deveined. Generously add salt plus a little pepper,
drizzle with a generous amount of oil and let stand for 5 minutes.

PREHEAT grill, barbecue or frying pan to high heat.

USE a long rectangular plate and Japanese or Chinese porcelain
soup spoon for each diner. Place a spoon on the left side of each
plate, and place a spot prawn on each spoon. Whisk the orange and
oil marinade until it has emulsified. Place a small amount in each
spoon with prawn and top with ½ teaspoon of the roasted tomatoes.
Place 1 tablespoon of the raw tomatoes in the middle of each plate.

GRILL scampi until just firm, remembering to use enough oil that
they don't stick to the cooking surface. Place on the right side of each
plate and finish with a light drizzle of oil. Serve immediately, and eat
from left to right.

BLACK PEPPER SQUID

SOLANGE HUYNH, *Phnom Penh Restaurant*

I was born in Cambodia, but when I was thirteen my family had to flee to Vietnam. When we first crossed over the border, we lived for a month and a half in the jungle, and eventually made our way to my aunt's house. Four years later we were still in Vietnam, except my brother. He had landed in Canada a couple of months earlier by boat and had won refugee status, but we didn't know if we would ever see him again. I met a Canadian immigration officer, Mr. René, while working as an interpreter, and he opened the door to Canada for us. I still thank him for giving our family a chance. In 1979, we started our new life in Canada, which was a very strange experience for us. My four sisters, two brothers, mother, father and grandmother all worked at various jobs, including gardening and ironing clothes in a factory. A few years later, on weekends, we started serving homemade noodles in Chinatown. We didn't have a permit and struggled a lot, but we never gave up. After two years, in 1985, we established Phnom Penh Restaurant legally and our hopes were fulfilled. Our grandmother always encouraged our family to keep the *power of love*. She gave us many traditional recipes and that's why we called the food in our menu "grandmother recipes." Phnom Penh serves a mixture of Cambodian, Chinese and Vietnamese cuisines, mirroring our family's origins. We also incorporate new ideas into our classic recipes such as Black Pepper Squid, a favourite that was created by my mother.

1 lb fresh or frozen
    filleted squid
1 Tbsp vegetable oil
½ onion, shredded
1 Tbsp fish sauce
2 Tbsp granulated sugar
pepper, to taste

› SERVES 4

CUT squid into 2-inch-wide strips and then cut a cross-hatch pattern into the surface. Bring a pot of water to a rolling boil and drop squid in. Boil for 3 minutes and strain, then pat dry.

HEAT oil in a frying pan over medium-high heat and brown onion for 1 minute. Add squid, fish sauce, sugar, and a lot of pepper and stir well for 2 minutes. Serve with rice or your choice of accompaniment.

BOO CHIM GAE

(SEAFOOD PANCAKE)

LUCIA KIM

Boo chim gae is a traditional South Korean dish. It has been in my family for generations, and I would think in other Korean families as well. It was one of the dishes that my mother taught me when I was a young girl. My mother came from a small farming town named Yaesan in South Korea, and it was not the richest town in the country. Her family farmed for a living. Everyone in the family worked the farm, including the kids. Being the oldest girl in the family, my mother cooked for the family as well. Maybe that is why she is such a good cook, and she has passed the tradition on to me. Back then, we would only make boo chim gae for big festivals and special family occasions because it was considered a delicacy in Yaesan. Nowadays, boo chim gae is very common, popular and affordable. You can find it in many South Korean restaurants. However, I still prefer to make it at home for my family to enjoy, because it reminds me of my mother and it brings back fond childhood memories.

> SERVES 4–6

SAUCE Mix all sauce ingredients well and add chili if desired. Put the sauce in a small serving bowl and set aside.

PANCAKES Whisk flour, water and salt in a bowl until the batter is smooth. Add green onions, carrot and all of the seafood. Put beaten eggs in the bowl and mix well.

HEAT 2 tablespoons of the oil in a pan. Put ½ cup of batter into the hot pan for each pancake and cook until it turns golden brown. Flip and cook the other side until it is well cooked. Add more oil as necessary while cooking pancakes. Placed cooked pancakes on a tray lined with paper towels. Repeat until you use all the batter. A 12-inch frying pan allows you to cook 3 pancakes at one time. This recipe makes about twenty-two 4-inch pancakes. Serve pancakes hot and pass the sauce.

SAUCE
4 Tbsp light soy sauce
1 Tbsp white vinegar
fresh chopped chili, to taste
  (optional)

PANCAKES
2 cups all-purpose flour
2½ cups water
1 tsp salt
1 bunch green onions, washed,
  dried and thinly sliced
½ carrot, peeled and finely
  julienned
4 oz cooked baby shrimp,
  chopped
4 oz shucked fresh oysters,
  cut into small pieces
4 oz squid, cleaned and patted
  dry, cut into small pieces
3 large eggs, beaten
½ cup oil, divided

PORK DUMPLINGS
WITH CHINESE CHIVES

CYNTHIA LI

To me, dumplings are always the best food I can think of whenever we are making food to share. They are the most important traditional food in China. We have them to celebrate the Spring Festival all over the country. They are a symbol of families gathering together and celebrating. Plus, they are delicious! Usually it is hard to make a dish that meets everyone's taste, but with dumplings you can, simply by putting in different fillings. How much dumplings are liked is well expressed in the old Chinese saying "Nothing is tastier than dumplings." However, what I like most is the fun of making dumplings together. We work as a team. Some people make the dumpling wrappings, while others wrap the dumplings. We sit relaxed around the table, talking while our hands do the work. After co-operating to make the dish, we all enjoy our accomplishment that includes everyone's efforts. We share the joy as well as the delicious food. Making dumplings is a really good way to communicate, co-operate and share with people. That is why I love to do it with family and friends, time and time again.

SAUCE
¼ cup light soy sauce
2 Tbsp rice vinegar
1 tsp sesame oil

DOUGH
2½ cups all-purpose flour
¾ cup water

FILLING
½ lb minced pork
½ tsp light soy sauce
½ tsp salt
dash of pepper
1 tsp sesame oil
½ tsp cornstarch
1 cup washed, dried and
    minced Chinese chives

> MAKES ABOUT 36 PIECES

SAUCE: Mix ingredients together. Pour into tiny bowls to be set at each place. Note: You may alter the proportions of this sauce to suit your taste.

DOUGH: In a large bowl, mix flour and water together with a fork until the mixture begins to hold together. Gather the mixture into a ball and knead gently into a smooth, soft dough. Cover with a damp cloth and set aside for 30 minutes.

FILLING: In a medium-sized bowl, mix pork with soy sauce, salt, pepper, sesame oil and cornstarch. Add chives and mix thoroughly. Set aside.

TO ASSEMBLE, sprinkle some flour on the table and use your hands to roll the dough out into a long sausage shape. Cut in half. Cover one half with a damp towel and set aside. Cut the other half into about 18 pieces. Flatten each piece with a rolling pin to make a thin square about 2¾ inches wide. Have a small bowl of water nearby. Place 1 well-rounded teaspoon of filling on each square. Using your fingertip, lightly dampen the edge of the dough with water. Bring opposite corners to meet each other in the centre, enclosing the filling, and press the edges to seal well, forming dumplings. Repeat with the remaining dough and filling.

BRING a large pot of water to a boil. Place the dumplings in and bring the water to a boil again. Add 1 to 2 cups of cold water, which will stop the boiling, and cook until it boils again. Repeat this step one more time. Total cooking time is about 15 minutes. When the dumplings are done they are fork-tender. Remove with a slotted spoon and serve with sauce.

› SPRING ROLLS

VICKY TZU-LUN FENG

I grew up in Taiwan and am currently a student at UBC in the Faculty of Arts. My family makes this recipe during a festival in mid-May when we honour our ancestors, but we sometimes make it during Lunar New Year too. My sister and I tend to fold our pancakes into envelopes or make them like dumplings, but my parents just roll them up. I like to imagine all of my ancestors standing or sitting around the table, choosing their favourite ingredients to put into their individual rolls.

› SERVES 6, WITH SOME LEFTOVER PANCAKES

PANCAKES: Place flour in a mixing bowl and gradually stir in water, mixing to make a stiff dough. When the dough is cool enough to handle, knead on a lightly floured surface until smooth and elastic (up to 10 minutes). Place the dough in a bowl, cover with a dish towel and let rest for 30 minutes.

PUT sesame oil in a small bowl. Place the dough on a lightly floured surface and roll out to ¼-inch thickness. Cut into rounds with a 3-inch cutter. With your fingers, daub a small amount of oil on top of 1 round. Place another round on top and press together. Roll out the 2 rounds together to form a circle about 6 or 7 inches in diameter. Cover with a damp kitchen cloth until ready to cook, and repeat with the remaining dough.

HEAT a large non-stick frying pan over medium heat. Cook 1 pancake at a time until barely golden and dry on both sides, turning once (about 1 minute total). Remove from the pan. When cool enough to handle, carefully separate the 2 pancakes. Wrap in foil until ready to use, or refrigerate. (To reheat, place in a steamer insert and steam, covered, for 5 minutes.) Makes about 20 to 24 pancakes.

PANCAKES

2 cups all-purpose flour
1 cup boiling water
2 Tbsp sesame oil

FILLING

six 6-inch strips of cucumber
2 Tbsp rice vinegar
dash of salt
2 cups chicken stock plus
   2 cups water or 4 cups water
1 lb boneless pork loin, cut
   into thin strips
6 large prawns, shelled
   and deveined
1 tsp salt
1 tsp granulated sugar
4 oz firm tofu, sliced into
   6 thin strips
vegetable oil for frying
5 oz bean sprouts
chopped cilantro (about 1 cup)
chopped roasted peanuts
   (about ¾ cup)

FILLING: Lightly pickle cucumber strips in rice vinegar and a dash of salt for a few minutes, then drain. Bring water and chicken stock to a boil in a large pot. Add strips of pork and simmer until almost cooked through, then add prawns and simmer until prawns are opaque. Drain. Mix prawns and pork with salt and sugar. Fry tofu in a hot frying pan with vegetable oil until golden brown.

TO SERVE, place pancakes on a serving plate. Arrange pork, prawns, tofu, sprouts and cucumber on a large platter. Set out bowls of cilantro and peanuts. To assemble the spring rolls, each person can place pancakes on a plate, then layer on small servings of the filling ingredients. Top with cilantro and roasted peanuts, roll up and eat!

⟩ GYOZA

JUSTIN AND LEA AULT, *Hapa Izakaya*

Gyoza are a Japanese adaptation of Chinese pot-stickers. During my time in Japan I would often have lunch at an all-gyoza restaurant in the Ginza neighbourhood of Tokyo. There were a dozen different types of gyoza to choose from, everything from super-spicy, to chicken, pork or beef, to cheese, vegetable and so on, with a variety of different sauces, though the traditional sauce is a vinegar and soy sauce. I also fell in love with Japanese homestyle cooking in general. Lea, my wife, learned to make gyoza, among other Japanese family dishes, from her mother. My mother-in-law made gyoza occasionally for her family, and more frequently when they began to take in Japanese students. The students enjoyed Western food but were happy to have homestyle Japanese food and often brought their friends over for Japanese meals. One female student had such an appetite for gyoza that she could eat thirty at one sitting. It's nice to be able to have Japanese family meals at home, and gyoza is a typical dish that we enjoy with just plain rice and a steamed vegetable.

⟩ SERVES 4

FILLING

1 lb ground pork
10 oz cabbage, boiled, drained, cooled and finely minced
2 Tbsp chopped green onion
1 Tbsp finely grated fresh ginger
2 Tbsp soy sauce (Japanese style)
1½ tsp salt

dumpling or wonton wrappers
water
unflavoured oil for frying (such as canola, peanut or vegetable)

DIPPING SAUCE

1 part rice vinegar
1 part soy sauce
chili oil or shichimi (Japanese chili-pepper condiment) or cayenne pepper, to taste

FILLING: Combine all filling ingredients in a bowl and set aside.

TO ASSEMBLE dumplings, you need an area to shape them, a wax-paper-lined baking sheet or plate for the finished dumplings, your wrappers (if using wonton wrappers, trim to make them round), a small dish of water and a Q-tip. Cover the wrappers with a damp cloth to keep them from drying out.

PLACE about 2 teaspoons of filling in the centre of a wrapper. Dip the Q-tip in water and run it along the perimeter of the wrapper to moisten. Draw the edges to meet in the middle over the filling. Press the edges together and crimp into tight pleats to seal completely. Continue until the gyoza is completely sealed. Four to five pleats should be sufficient to give you a crescent-shaped dumpling that sits on its bottom with the pleated edge pointing straight up on top. Set aside on a wax-paper-lined baking sheet or plate. Continue until you run out of filling or wrappers. We generally allow for about 10 gyoza per person, or 5 to 6 if you are serving other dishes. This recipe will feed about 4 people.

HEAT either a frying pan or an electric frying pan (make sure it has a lid) over medium-high heat until water droplets shaken onto it bounce. If the water disappears in a puff of vapour, it's too hot. Add about 3 tablespoons oil to the pan and tilt the pan so that oil covers the surface thinly. Working quickly, lay out the gyoza in rows in the pan. Let fry, checking to make sure they don't get too brown. When the bottoms are golden brown, add about ¼ cup water to the pan and cover. Let steam for about 5 minutes. Lift out carefully. Serve immediately, with steamed Japanese rice, dipping sauce and some vegetables. We like a plain steamed vegetable such as spinach with this meal as the gyoza are very flavourful.

DIPPING SAUCE: We usually use equal parts rice vinegar and soy sauce and let people add their own chili oil or shichimi, but it can also be mixed ahead of time according to taste.

EMPANADAS

ESTHER REVES

The great variety of robust flavours found throughout Argentina may very well be summed up in the savoury delight known as the empanada. These popular meat pastries vary slightly in every geographic locale and every household, ensuring a treasure chest of surprise every time you eat one. I have munched on them in the cafés of Buenos Aires, fried, where they are a handy fast food; I have shared the baked, trendy take-out style with my cousin's family in the city, and I have enjoyed them hot out of the oven, made with chicken, loads of parsley and touches of tomato, in the quiet northern country of the dry Chaco. But my fondest memory is making them with my aunt in Resistencia. Homemade ones are the best and are reserved for special occasions. But the time they take to prepare goes quickly when shared in good company and in the anticipation of reward as the end result. Making the pastry from scratch is best done ahead of time. The filling may also be made a day in advance. There's nothing quite like having a day to devote to making them fresh, savouring the smells that waft from every stage of preparation. I usually make these empanadas as appetizers around Christmas and New Year's, for parties and my family. They are always a hit and always bring memories of my aunt and relatives, so far away. They are a culinary tie that binds me to my father's homeland, for which I have immense love.

PASTRY

1 cup cream cheese,
   room temperature
1 cup unsalted butter,
   room temperature
2¼ cups all-purpose flour
pinch of salt

FILLING

1 lb lean ground beef
1 large onion, minced
1–3 cloves garlic, minced
½–¾ cup canned tomatoes,
   with their juice, chopped
2–4 Tbsp chopped dark raisins
2–4 Tbsp chopped green olives
1–2 tsp dried oregano
1–2 tsp dried basil
salt and pepper, to taste
2–3 eggs, hard-cooked,
   chopped

1 egg, beaten (for sealing
   pastry and brushing tops
   before baking)

> MAKES ABOUT 55 PIECES

PASTRY: Blend cream cheese and butter together in a large bowl. Add flour and salt and mix thoroughly. Gather the pastry dough into a ball. Dust lightly with flour and flatten into a disk shape. Wrap in wax paper and chill 1 hour before rolling out.

FILLING: Heat a large frying pan over medium-high heat. Add beef and brown, breaking it up with a wooden spoon. Drain off most of the fat, add onion and brown well. Add garlic and sauté briefly. Add enough tomatoes so that mixture is still thick, yet juicy and not dry. Stir in remaining ingredients except for eggs; simmer, stirring frequently, for 5 minutes or until most of the juice is gone. Remove from heat and cool slightly so it thickens. Stir in chopped eggs. (At this point, the mixture may be covered and refrigerated overnight.)

ASSEMBLY: Preheat the oven to 400°F.

On a lightly floured surface, roll pastry to ⅛-inch thickness and cut into rounds, 2½ to 3 inches in diameter. Place a teaspoonful of the meat mixture just off centre on each round and brush egg wash around the edges to help seal. Fold pastry over filling and press edges together well or they'll pop open while baking. Brush tops with egg wash if you wish, and cut a small slit in each.

Being in a health-conscious country, we bake the empanadas 12 to 15 minutes (rather than frying them) until nicely browned. Superb served at any temperature.

BRIOCHE AUX ESCARGOTS

MANUEL FERREIRA, *Le Gavroche*

Growing up in a traditional European family in Portugal and France, I learned at an early age the appreciation of fresh food and fine wines. Studying to be an engineer, I transferred to Montreal in 1976 to work on the Expo site. When that project ended, I began my culinary career in the kitchen, receiving on-the-job training. After two years I moved to the front of the house and put my love of hospitality and wine to better use. Eventually I found my way to Vancouver and to Le Gavroche. I started as restaurant manager, then became a partner, and in 1994 became the owner.

This recipe from Portugal is a traditional peasant bread that my mother made all the time. When we were really busy with the harvest in the fall and there was no time to sit down and eat, we could always run into the kitchen and she would have a loaf of this bread staying warm on top of the stove so we could cut off a big piece and head back out to the fields. I also fondly remember searching through the orchards and fields every fall collecting the snails!

> MAKES 1 LOAF

PREHEAT the oven to 375°F.

ESCARGOTS: In a frying pan, heat butter over medium heat and sauté escargots with parsley, shallot and garlic for about 3 minutes and let cool at room temperature.

BRIOCHE: Sift flour and sugar into a mixing bowl. Combine yeast and water, allow yeast to proof and add to flour. Blend the mixture with a dough hook at low speed. Add eggs one at a time until combined. Add butter cubes one at a time. Add salt and mix for 10 minutes. Mix escargots into dough. Fill a buttered loaf pan three-quarters full with dough and cover with slightly damp towel. Let rise for 1 hour. Bake until golden brown (about 45 minutes). Serve warm.

ESCARGOTS
4 Tbsp butter
24 escargots, well rinsed
1 cup finely chopped parsley
1 shallot, finely minced
2 cloves garlic, finely minced

BRIOCHE
3½ cups all-purpose flour
2 Tbsp granulated sugar
2 tsp active dry yeast
  (⅔ envelope)
½ cup warm water (follow
  yeast package instructions
  for proofing)
5 large eggs
1 cup unsalted butter,
  cut into 15 cubes,
  at room temperature
2 tsp kosher salt

> LEFSE

(POTATO FLAT BREAD)

JOAN CROSS

My grandmother's lefse recipe connects me with my Norwegian heritage and the grandparents I didn't have the privilege of meeting. While growing up here, our family took occasional summer car trips to the Prairies to visit numerous aunts, uncles and cousins. As soon as Mom and her five sisters got together they spoke Norwegian and started cooking. We kids didn't appreciate every dish but lefse was a hit. Over the years my mother, Clara, and I have made many batches of lefse together, especially at Christmas. My favourite filling to roll up in this flat bread is shaved cheese, but it is equally good spread with butter and your favourite jam or sprinkled with sugar. And a cup of strong coffee, of course.

2 lb russet potatoes
(about 4 large), peeled
1¼ tsp salt
2 Tbsp butter, softened
1 Tbsp cream, either whipping
cream or half-and-half
all-purpose flour
(about 2 cups), plus more
for rolling out dough

> MAKES 16 PIECES

CUT potatoes roughly and place in a saucepan. Add cold water, just enough to cover. Bring to a boil, reduce heat and simmer until tender. Drain. Push potatoes through a ricer or a food mill (or you could make them very smooth with a potato masher). You should have 4½ to 5 cups.

PUT potatoes into a large bowl. With a wooden spoon, stir in salt, butter and cream and then add flour gradually. As you stir the dough will form into a ball and no longer feel sticky.

TURN out onto a well-floured surface. Break off 16 pieces, each the size of a small orange. Pat a piece into a circle, dusting with flour to prevent sticking. Roll into a circle, about ⅛ inch thick and 6 inches in diameter (see note). Repeat with remaining pieces.

HEAT an electric frying pan or griddle to 350°F or use a non-stick pan over medium heat. (There is no need to oil the pan.) Cook each piece about 1 minute per side or until golden-brown spots appear all over.

NOTE An easier approach to this recipe is to roll the lefse a little thicker, in which case the yield would be about 12 pieces.

‹ BABETTES

GAIL NEFF BELL

The women of my many-generations-Canadian family have always baked bread, so it was natural that when my mother came back from seeing the amazing sights of Paris she brought back a new idea about bread—that it should be long and slender, and be baked on a sheet rather than in a loaf pan. She called the bread she made to this new standard a babette. Eating a babette with our soup made us feel very elegant.

There have been changes over the years. Mum eventually found out that the word she had heard as babette is pronounced *baguette!* Then the food processor and some new baking techniques made this treat easy to make. Finally I realized that while it's great with soup, it's even better as a platform for appetizers. I make it extremely slender, so that each slice is just a couple of bites, and I top the slices with sweet butter and the best cheddar, or my neighbour's cold-smoked salmon, or curried chicken and a dab of pear chutney, or any other delicious thing that comes to mind. But whatever I top it with, and whatever others may call this French bread, to me it is and always will be my mother's babette.

1 cup water, very warm but not hot
2½ cups unbleached flour, divided
1 tsp traditional dry yeast
1 tsp salt
½ cup cake flour
1 egg, beaten with a pinch of salt

‹ MAKES 2–3 LOAVES

POUR all but a spoonful of the water into the food processor bowl with the steel blade installed. Add 1 cup of the unbleached flour. Pulse once or twice, just so you get a slurry. Sprinkle yeast on top and use the rest of the water to moisten the yeast. Let yeast dissolve for about 5 minutes, then add salt, cake flour and the rest of the unbleached flour. Pulse the food processor several times until the dough forms a firm ball.

PLACE the dough on a floured board and knead a few times until it's a smooth ball. Place in a large oiled bowl, turning to coat the dough with oil. Cover the bowl with a tea towel and allow the dough to rise until double in volume (about 1½ hours) in a warm, draft-free place beside a bowl of steaming water (the microwave is a good place).

ON a floured surface, punch the dough down and roll into 2 or 3 long ropes as big around as the base of your thumb and about 14 inches long. Place on a baking sheet. Let them rise in a warm, draft-free place containing a bowl of steaming water until they are double in size.

PREHEAT the oven to 400°F.

BRUSH the tops of the loaves with egg mixture. Bake for about 20 minutes. When they're done, they will sound hollow when tapped.

NESSIE'S OATMEAL SCONES

CANDACE KNIGHTON

My grandmother Nessie was born in Scotland. She was one of many children in a family with little money. She immigrated to Canada when she was eighteen, married shortly thereafter and had four children. Her husband died at the beginning of the Depression, which left her with few resources to bring up her young family so she was always frugal and "made do."

Many years later, when she had money, she still cooked like she didn't. When I'd go to visit her I would always hope she had just baked scones, rather than having other, less palatable treats on the table. Her own version of headcheese or Turkish delight was almost impossible to choke down.

Her scones, however, were fabulous, especially during raspberry season. She'd send me out to the rows of canes, which were lovingly tended by husband number three, to get enough raspberries for afternoon tea. I ate as many berries as I picked. My worried grandpa would hover and gasp if he felt I was damaging next year's canes, but he gently tolerated the hordes of Nessie's grandchildren who helped themselves to the product of his labours.

I'd return to the house with the berries. The smell of the warm scones permeated the air. Before I could eat, Grandma would take me into the bathroom and scrub down my hands and neck with a bristle brush. She was a firm believer in cleanliness but also, I feel, enjoyed making her grandchildren suffer a bit before pleasure. The stinging neck was worth it when I'd eat those great scones all slathered with homemade raspberry jam. I would stick the fresh berries on top of the jam and bite. Heaven.

When my own children were little I'd make Grandma's scones every Sunday morning for breakfast. It is rare now for any of us to eat breakfast together, so scones are saved for afternoon teas with my friends. I embellish them with homemade Saltspring Island blackberry jam. I think Nessie would approve.

1¼ cups all-purpose flour
¼ cup ground rolled oats (pulverized in food processor) or use oat flour
1½ tsp baking powder
½ tsp baking soda
1 Tbsp granulated sugar
pinch of salt
¼ cup each of cold butter, cubed, and shortening or use ½ cup cold unsalted butter, cubed
½–¾ cup buttermilk
sugar for sprinkling on top

PREHEAT the oven to 425°F. In a large bowl mix together all dry ingredients. With a pastry blender or knife, cut butter and shortening (or butter) into the dry mixture until the dough is roughly the texture of peas. Using a fork, stir in enough buttermilk to hold the mixture together (it shouldn't be sticky). Turn dough out onto a floured board and knead 3 to 4 times. Pat dough into a round about 1 inch thick and place it on a baking sheet that has been lined with parchment paper. Cut the round into 6 to 8 wedges (keep the wedges together in a circle). Sprinkle with sugar. Bake for 15 to 20 minutes until brown. Eat immediately with preserves and Devon cream.

GRANDMA YERBURY'S WELSH CAKES

MARIE FRASER

My mother was born in South Wales in a coal-mining village in the Rhonda Valley. In August of 1914, Grandma and Grandpa and their eight children came to live in Fernie. When they arrived they found that the mine had gone on strike, so Grandpa joined the Canadian army. After the war, the family obtained a farm in Lister, a "soldiers' settlement" close to Creston. Each winter, they closed up the farm and Grandpa went to work in the mills at Ocean Falls. My sister and I looked forward to having Grandma come and spend her winters visiting the families of her three daughters in Kimberley. Along with her suitcases, she always brought her heavy, blackened griddle in anticipation of our demand for Welsh cakes! I remember cold winter days spent sitting in the wicker rocker with my feet warming on the hot-water reservoir of our wood stove, waiting for the first of those currant-filled cakes to come off the griddle. My own cast-iron griddle shows signs of wear after years of frying the cakes to add to the care packages going off to my children in their first years away from home.

3 cups all-purpose flour
3 tsp baking powder
½ tsp salt
¼ tsp nutmeg
1 cup granulated sugar
½ cup unsalted butter, cold and cubed, plus more for cooking
1 cup currants, picked over for stems, washed and dried
2 large eggs, lightly beaten
½ cup milk, plus more for mixing dough
1 tsp vanilla extract

> MAKES THIRTY-SIX 3-INCH CAKES

COMBINE flour, baking powder, salt, nutmeg and sugar in a large bowl. Using a wire pastry blender, cut in the butter until the mixture is crumbly. Stir in currants. In a small bowl, mix eggs, milk and vanilla together, then add to the flour mixture. Using a fork, mix just until the dough begins to hold together (you may need to add a bit more milk). Gather the dough into a ball. Flatten the ball and roll on a lightly floured surface to ¼-inch thickness. Cut into 2- to 3-inch rounds. Re-roll scraps and cut into rounds. Add a small amount of butter to a griddle or frying pan over medium heat. (Not too hot— lower heat than you need to cook pancakes.) Cook cakes in batches until browned on both sides, about 2 to 3 minutes per side. The cakes can be served hot or cold.

SEVILLE ORANGE MARMALADE

LOUISE ALLIX

My grandmother was born in Orillia, in what was then called Upper Canada, in 1844. After marrying my English grandfather she returned with him to Yorkshire and raised a family; my father was their second son. I just remember her as a very old lady, dressed in deepest black and knitting. She died at the age of ninety-six in 1940. My grandparents lived in some style—nowadays we would call it luxury—and I'm sure Granny never cooked anything in her life; after all, what were cooks for? So it is a bit mysterious that I have inherited several recipes from her, including one for green tomato chutney that makes enough for a small army, and another for the best orange marmalade in the world. I make this marmalade every January when the Seville oranges appear, and the jars of it are extremely popular gifts.

6 Seville oranges
1 lemon
water
granulated sugar (as much as 10 cups, see below)

> MAKES TEN TO TWELVE 8-OZ JARS

SQUEEZE oranges and lemon and measure the juice. Remove pips and tie them in a cheesecloth bag. Remove pulp and set aside, then finely slice rind. Increase juice to 12 cups with cold water and pour over rind, pulp and pips in a large pot. Soak for 24 to 48 hours, covered, at room temperature.

BRING the mixture to a boil, then reduce heat and simmer gently for 2 to 3 hours, until the rind is soft. Remove the bag of pips and cool. Squeeze out well into a clean bowl—this produces a kind of gel that is important because it contains pectin. Measure all of the pulp, rind and juice in the pot and for each cup add 1 cup of sugar. Stir the gel into the marmalade mixture. Bring to a boil, stirring until sugar is completely dissolved. Boil hard for about 20 minutes. (I usually divide it between two pans as it needs room to bubble up.) Test until done. (To test, put a little marmalade on a cold saucer—if it wrinkles when you push it with your finger, it is done.) Follow proper canning procedure to finish.

KRISHNA JAMAL'S PUMPKIN-GINGER CHUTNEY

SHAFFEEN JAMAL, *Tamarind*

I was born in Tanzania, where my great-grandfather ended up after stowing away on a ship at the tender age of nine. Due to the political situation in that country, our family moved to England when I was seven. In our new country, my family went into the restaurant business with partners, and our first place was a Greek coffee shop in a predominantly Irish neighbourhood. The menu was English comfort food—lots of meat and potatoes! Eight months later we decided to strike out on our own and bought a restaurant called Rubina Grill in another part of town. This restaurant also served English food, but within two years my mother, Chef Krishna Jamal, had reinvented the menu with her own Indian specialties, with influences from our family's roots in India and Africa. In 1983, we moved to Canada and opened Rubina Tandoori in East Vancouver on Canada Day. In 2004, we opened our latest venture, Tamarind Bistro. This pumpkin-ginger chutney is an old family favourite that I liked to spread on hot toast in the morning when I was growing up. I used to complain to Mom about the ginger, asking her to leave it out. But she would tell me that it was good for me—the ginger fights off colds.

> MAKES 12 CUPS

4 lb cleaned pumpkin, peeled and cut into ½-inch chunks
1 large red onion, finely chopped
1 apple, peeled, cored and grated
1 pear, cored and finely chopped
3 oz yellow raisins
4 oz fresh ginger, grated
2½ cups granulated sugar (brown sugar works but changes the colour of the chutney)
1 cinnamon stick
pinch of ground cloves
pinch of ground cardamom
1 hot red chili pepper, seeded and finely chopped
1 tsp salt
1 tsp pepper
¾ cup cider vinegar
¾ cup canola oil

PUT all ingredients into a large stainless-steel pan and bring to a boil. Boil for 3 to 5 minutes, then simmer over low heat for 50 to 60 minutes. If it gets too dry, add a few tablespoons of water and, depending on the pumpkin, mash the flesh a little bit for a chunky texture. Remove the cinnamon stick.

PUT the chutney in clean hot jars and process according to correct canning method. Label once cold. Store the jars in a cool, dark place, and refrigerate once opened.

TOMATO CHUTNEY

TERENCE DAWSON

My family and I emigrated from England to Canada when I was five years old. To this day, when I return to England to visit relatives, I feel as though I am heading home. This chutney recipe is filled with things from the garden, and my grandparents' garden remains a vivid memory for me. Grandad made a lawn-bowling green beside it, and Nan and I would play bowls as he tended his garden of vegetables and flowers. One summer, he lost his signet ring amongst the runner beans. Years later, Nan was picking beans one morning and found it. It had grown up from beneath the ground on one of the beanstalks. I now wear that same ring. When I make this chutney, the recipe handed down from Nan, I somehow feel connected to the country of my birth and to those memories once again.

15 medium-sized ripe tomatoes (about 3 lb)
bowl of ice water for blanching
3 cups chopped apples
1 heaping cup raisins
3 large onions, chopped
2 tsp cinnamon
2 tsp dry mustard
1 tsp pepper
2 Tbsp salt
1 tsp ground cloves
2 cups malt vinegar or apple cider vinegar
2 cups packed brown sugar

> MAKES 8 CUPS

CUT a small × into the blossom end of each tomato. Bring a large pot of water to a boil and blanch tomatoes in boiling water for about 25 seconds to loosen their skins. Plunge into a bowl of ice water and the skins will slip off easily. Chop up tomatoes (including core) roughly.

IN a large saucepan, stir together all the ingredients and let stand for 1 hour. Bring the mixture to a boil, reduce heat and cook slowly over low heat for 2 hours, stirring occasionally.

PLACE the chutney in hot jars and process according to correct canning method. Or you can store it in freshly sterilized jars in the refrigerator for up to 3 months. Or give it out to friends!

› GARLIC PICKLE

MICHAEL KAWESKI

I was on an eye-opening, life-changing nine-month trip around the world in 1988–89 when I picked up this recipe in southern India. While in Kerala, a friend and I spent several days in the Cardamom Hills. The name was very descriptive, as the main street of the small town we stayed in was fragrant with the cardamom harvest, and we watched men deliberately haggling around huge piles of deep-green pods. From the hills, we travelled down to the historic spice-trading port of Cochin, where an international spice festival was taking place. The displays were quaint, but the staff were enthusiastic, and in the evening there was an entertaining enactment of the founding of trade with Europe and a stunning performance of Kathakali dance. I picked up several recipe cards there. I make this recipe for garlic pickle annually, from my harvest of Russian red garlic from the backyard and a mix of Stein Mountain Farm's hot chilies from the East Van Farmers' Market. The recipe changes a bit every year as I try out different chilies, vinegars, oils and sweeteners. We love it on simple grain and pulse dishes, along with oil and yogurt, or with Indian meals. For quick snacks we'll mix it with mayo and spread it on toast. Making this pickle each fall and enjoying it throughout the year will always bring back satisfying memories of that great trip.

2¾ lb garlic
7 Tbsp granulated sugar
10 Tbsp salt
4 tsp turmeric
2⅛ cups freshly squeezed lime juice (about 4½ lb limes)
⅞ cup vegetable oil
2 tsp asafoetida powder (also known as *hing*)—available in Indian or Southeast Asian markets
5¼ oz fresh chilies, well washed and dried
10 Tbsp chopped fresh ginger
6 Tbsp mustard powder
5 Tbsp red chili powder
7 Tbsp white vinegar

› MAKES ABOUT 2 LITRES

PEEL and chop garlic. Mix with sugar, salt, turmeric and lime juice. Set aside for 1 hour in the refrigerator (see note).

HEAT oil in a frying pan over high heat. Fry asafoetida, chilies, ginger and mustard powder until chilies soften and the mixture is very fragrant. Cool and add chili powder.

MIX fried seasonings with garlic mixture. Add vinegar. Place the garlic pickle in clean, covered containers and refrigerate for 6 to 7 days to cure before use. Store in the refrigerator for up to 6 months. If you want to store it longer, process according to proper canning method.

NOTE Chopped garlic can develop harmful pathogens if left at room temperature. Cut only what you will use and set it aside in the refrigerator very briefly if necessary.

> SOUPS, SALADS

and SIDE DISHES

SUJEBI

(SOUP WITH WHEAT FLAKES)

SEORAN LEE

In winter, sujebi is a favourite Korean dish. It's easy and enjoyable to make with the family. My mom cooked it for us when I was young, and I have memories of the whole family sitting around the table, making the dough into many shapes, talking and eating together. My mom would tell me sad stories from the past. After the Korean War, the economic situation was so bad that the majority of the people suffered in poverty. They couldn't even eat rice as their staple food, so that's how sujebi was discovered. Although sujebi is a food that reminds people of poverty, it really is delicious and I love it!

> SERVES 3–4

DOUGH

3 cups whole wheat flour
  or white flour
1 Tbsp oil
pinch of salt
1 cup warm water

SOUP

6 cups water *or* use 6 cups fish,
  chicken or beef stock and
  omit anchovies
7 anchovies
1 Tbsp minced garlic
pinch of salt
pinch of pepper
½ cup sliced green onions
½ cup julienned zucchini

DOUGH: Measure flour into a large bowl. Combine oil and salt with flour, using a fork. Stir in warm water and then knead the dough into a slightly sticky ball. Cover the dough with plastic wrap to lock in the moisture and refrigerate for 1 hour. Remove from refrigerator and allow to rest 15 minutes.

SOUP: Bring 6 cups of water and anchovies (or stock) to a boil. If using water and anchovies, strain into a clean saucepan and discard any bits of anchovy (most of them melt into the broth) and bring back to a boil. Tear off pieces of dough (any size you want) and place in the boiling broth. Add garlic, salt and pepper. Cover the pot and simmer until the pieces of dough are cooked (the time will depend on the size you choose to make them). Taste a piece after 10 minutes and cook further if needed. Add green onions and zucchini, cover and heat for 2 to 3 minutes.

This is the basic soup; you can add meat, an egg swirl and other veggies.

SOUPE AUX MOULES DE MAMIE SUZANNE

JEAN FRANCIS QUAGLIA, *Provence Restaurants*

This soup is one of my favourite childhood memories from my mother's kitchen in Marseille. That memory came to life when my mother came to cook it for our patrons in our restaurants, and now it has become a fond memory of theirs too! I didn't really know how she made it until she came to Vancouver for the first time and I had a chance to watch her. Now I make it at home and hope it creates as many memories for my sons as my mother's did for me. This recipe is somewhat labour-intensive and quite costly, but the result is sublime! It's a meal in itself that would be great after a day of skiing or hiking. It can also be made a day in advance.

> SERVES 10

MUSSELS: In a large stockpot, steam mussels with all ingredients. After mussels open, remove from heat. Separate mussels from the juice. Strain the juice into a container and set aside—*do not discard the mussel liquid!* Discard any mussels that do not open. Count out enough whole mussels for garnish, about 3 to 4 per person. The rest can be removed from their shells, puréed and set aside.

SOUP: Melt butter in your stockpot and add garlic, onion and parsley. Sweat gently but do not colour. Add bay leaves and fennel. Mix in tomato paste and the puréed mussels. Sprinkle flour over the mixture and stir, then pour in the mussel liquid and cooking wine. Allow to simmer over medium heat for about 15 to 20 minutes. Now add saffron. Allow to simmer for another 10 minutes. Check the seasoning—you will probably need some salt and pepper. Taste after each addition of salt and pepper to get it just right.

SERVE the soup with reserved whole mussels and, if desired, garlic-rubbed croutons, and a little crème fraîche. Don't forget to close your eyes and imagine you are in the South of France!

MUSSELS

6 lb fresh mussels, cleaned
   and beards removed
4 cups white cooking wine
½ bunch fresh parsley
2 dried fennel stalks *or* 1 small
   fennel bulb, chopped
1 large onion, chopped

SOUP

3 Tbsp butter
3 cloves garlic, chopped
1 large onion, chopped
1 bunch parsley, chopped
2 bay leaves
2 dried fennel stalks *or* 4 fresh
   fennel stalks, chopped
¼ cup tomato paste
¼ cup flour
1 cup white cooking wine
1½ tsp saffron

CHICKEN AVGOLEMONO SOUP

PAVLO LIAKAKOS

This soup is from Greece, my homeland and birth-place. My family and I immigrated to Canada in 1953, when I was the tender age of three. I'm still quite fluent in Greek, and many people ask, how did you learn? My answer to them is with a big wooden spoon. Many winter nights I looked forward to my mother's chicken avgolemono soup. This is a very simple recipe that can be prepared in a short time and be on the table in less than an hour. Cheers and bon appétit!

7½ cups chicken stock
½ cup orzo pasta
3 eggs
1 Tbsp cornstarch
⅓ cup cold water
juice of 1 lemon
salt and pepper, to taste
lemon slices for garnish

> SERVES 4–6

POUR stock into a large soup pot and bring to a boil. Add orzo pasta and cook for 12 minutes, or until pasta is tender.

BEAT eggs until frothy. Mix cornstarch, cold water and lemon juice until smooth, and stir into eggs. Very slowly whisk ½ cup of the hot stock into the egg-and-lemon mixture.

TAKE the soup off the heat and add the egg-lemon sauce to soup. Gently stir and add salt and pepper to taste. Return to heat and keep warm on the lowest heat. Garnish with lemon slices and serve.

NOTE *Do not* let the soup boil once the eggs have been added, as it will curdle!

ELEANORE'S BORSCHT

ELEANORE CROSS-SPRY

My parents came from Russia to homestead in Saskatchewan, and I was born and raised on the farm. Being the eldest daughter, I also helped my mother cook many dishes from her homeland. Our garden provided excellent produce, and my father baked bread for our large family—several round loaves at a time. Borscht, my favourite soup, is one of the dishes I've prepared for my own family.

> SERVES 12

NOTE Best started the day before serving.

BROTH: Place brisket and bones in a stockpot and cover with cold water. Bring to a boil over medium-high heat. Skim off foam as it rises. Once the surface is clear of foam, add onion and carrot. Add the bouquet garni, and salt. Reduce heat and simmer for 1½ hours or until meat is tender. When tender, remove meat and bones. Dice all meat and set aside. Return bones to the pot and continue cooking broth for up to 5 hours, until broth has a rich flavour. Strain, chill and remove fat.

SOUP: Heat oil in a large, heavy pot. Sauté onion and garlic until soft but not browned. Add half the tomatoes (mix the other half with the chopped meat and set aside) and 1½ cups broth. Then add beets, celery root, parsley root, parsnip, sugar, vinegar and salt. Simmer 40 minutes or until vegetables are tender.

MEANWHILE, add cabbage and potatoes to remaining broth, bring to a boil, reduce heat and simmer about 20 minutes, until potatoes are tender but not mushy.

COMBINE soup, cabbage-potato mixture and meat-tomato mixture. Cover partially and simmer about 15 minutes until heated through. Serve hot with individual bowls of sour cream, chopped parsley and chopped dill as garnishes.

BROTH
1 lb beef brisket
4–5 lb beef bones (ask butcher to crack them)
1 large onion, peeled and quartered
1 large carrot, peeled and quartered
1 bouquet garni: 3 celery tops, 1 bay leaf and 3 parsley stalks, tied together
1 Tbsp salt

SOUP
1 Tbsp vegetable oil
1 cup chopped onion
2 cloves garlic, finely chopped
4 tomatoes, peeled, seeded and chopped, divided
1 lb beets, tops off, peeled and grated (about 2 cups)
½ celery root, peeled and grated (about 1 cup)
1 parsley root (if possible), well washed
1 parsnip, peeled and grated (about 1 cup)
½ tsp granulated sugar
¼ cup red wine vinegar
1 Tbsp salt

1 lb cabbage, coarsely shredded
1 lb potatoes, peeled and diced

HAM AND BARLEY SOUP

MILENA ROBERTSON

As a child growing up in Ljubljana, Slovenia, we often used any leftover meats to make wholesome, rich soups. One of my favourites was a ham and barley soup made on those rare occasions when we had a ham bone available—truly a special treat. Nowadays, Christmas Eve in our home in Vancouver is celebrated with friends, international food and good wine. The main event is always a huge baked ham. Carrying on the tradition from my childhood, after all the festivities are over on Boxing Day, the ham bone and leftover meat are used to make this delicious soup.

> SERVES 6–8

COMBINE barley, ham bone, salt, a few grindings of pepper and water in a heavy 4- to 6-quart pot and bring to a boil over high heat. Reduce the heat to low, partially cover the pan and simmer for 45 minutes. Add leeks, celery, onion, potato and chicken stock and continue to simmer for 30 minutes, or until barley is soft and vegetables are tender. Remove ham bone, chop any ham meat and return meat to the soup. Discard ham bone. Stirring constantly, pour in cream in a slow stream and simmer for 2 to 3 minutes to heat the soup thoroughly. Taste for seasoning and add more salt and pepper if needed. Serve from a heated soup tureen or on individual soup plates.

½ cup pearl barley
1 ham bone with some meat left on it
1 tsp salt
pepper, to taste
10 cups cold water
1 cup finely chopped leeks, including 2 inches of the green tops
½ cup finely chopped celery
½ cup finely chopped onion
1 medium baking potato, peeled and finely chopped
one 10-oz can undiluted chicken stock
1 cup heavy cream

› PHO THAI

KIM THAI, *The Sutton Place Hotel*

I was born in Saigon but left Vietnam as a teenager with my brother and sister-in-law and escaped to a refugee camp in Malaysia. Life in the camp was pretty horrific, but one day consulate representatives from the United States, Britain and Canada interviewed us. We ended up coming to Canada because the Canadian consulate was the first to offer us the opportunity to emigrate. We had no idea what life would be like in Canada but we had one goal—to work hard, become citizens and earn enough money to bring the rest of our family to our new country. I had many low-paying jobs at first, but when I was working as a dishwasher in a little French fine-dining restaurant, I was given the chance to be the chef/owner's assistant. I had never cooked in my life before, but it was the opportunity that changed my life forever. Now, twenty years later, I'm the executive chef of the Sutton Place Hotel in Vancouver. Plus, my brother, sister-in-law and I have managed to sponsor our entire family to become Canadian citizens, and the whole family now calls Vancouver home! This is a traditional Vietnamese recipe, with a lot of French influence. My mother prepares it often—so often that she wasn't sure of the exact measurements, so we tested it in the hotel's kitchen with amazing results. Enjoy!

› SERVES 8

BROTH: In a large stockpot filled with boiling water, individually blanch oxtails, beef bones and shanks (if using) for 5 minutes. Remove and rinse thoroughly with cold water to remove any foam. Discard boiling water and refill stockpot with 24 cups cold water. Add oxtails, beef bones and shanks. Bring to a full boil, then immediately reduce the heat to simmer. Occasionally skim off any additional foam to prevent the stock from becoming cloudy.

MEANWHILE, char ginger and onion on a preheated element or broiler until they're lightly blackened on both sides (about 3 to 6 minutes),

BROTH

2 lb oxtails, cut into
  1½- to 2-inch pieces
2 lb beef stock bones
1 lb beef shanks (optional)
24 cups cold water
1 piece whole fresh ginger
  (about 4 oz), not peeled,
  lightly crushed
1 large onion, not peeled,
  cut in half
1½ lb daikon, cut into chunks
salt, to taste
¼ cup fish sauce, to taste

SACHET

5 whole star anise
5 whole cloves
2 cinnamon sticks,
  2 inches long
1½ tsp fennel seeds, lightly
  crushed
3 bay leaves

1 lb rice noodles, fresh or dried
1 lb raw, lean rib-eye beef,
  thinly sliced

then scrape off excess char and add onion and ginger to the stockpot. Tie the sachet spices in cheesecloth and add to the stockpot. After about 3 hours, take the shanks out and let them cool, then thinly slice the meat off the bones and refrigerate it. Discard bones. After about 5 hours add daikon and check seasoning. Season with salt and fish sauce to taste. By this time the broth should be incredibly flavourful and aromatic throughout the house and neighbourhood.

NOODLES: As the broth nears completion, soak rice noodles in cold water for at least 10 minutes (depending on the type of noodles—see package). You can then par-cook the noodles and reheat in the microwave when ready to serve, or boil noodles in a large pot of water. Give the noodles a quick stir and cook until tender but firm, about 1 minute only (don't let the noodles overcook, or you'll be left with a pile of stringy, gummy paste).

GARNISH: Place the warm noodles in large soup bowls and arrange the sliced raw beef, beef shank meat, bean sprouts and sliced white onions on top of the noodles. Carefully ladle the hot broth over it all, to about ½ inch above. Sprinkle with green onions, cilantro and pepper and serve immediately.

The technique is for each person to season his or her bowl of pho, by adding Thai basil, chilies, hoisin sauce, chili-garlic paste and fresh lime juice—this keeps the flavour bright and fresh. Each bowl is tailored to individual taste.

NOTE Oxtails can be served as a side dish for everyone to share, just like osso buco. Or, while making the broth, remove oxtails after 4 hours (when the meat is tender), cool, take the meat off and add to pho when serving.

This broth can also be made with chicken, as many people don't eat red meat.

GARNISH
1 lb fresh bean sprouts,
    raw or blanched
½ cup thinly sliced white onion
2 green onions, thinly sliced
½ bunch fresh cilantro leaves,
    roughly chopped (about 1 oz)
pepper
2 bunches Thai basil leaves
    (found in Asian markets)
hoisin sauce (optional)
chili-garlic paste (optional)
sliced fresh hot chilies
    (optional)
2 large limes, cut into wedges

UNCLE BILL'S OXTAIL MOCK TURTLE SOUP

JOYCE VANDEGRIEND

Great-uncle Bill jumped on a ship leaving Rotter-dam when he was twenty-one. In Canada, he landed a job as a camp cook in the middle of nowhere. He had my grandmother's (his sister's) recipes, and boy, could he cook! Later he prospected for gold. He lived a full life until 1995 and left me his Hardy cane fly-fishing rods, his binoculars with moose blood on them and his recipes. This is his Oxtail Mock Turtle Soup, originally from the Kooi-man Hotel in Rotterdam where Great-Grandfather Arthur Senior was a grain broker. The recipe calls for Madeira, and since Uncle Bill had been there, no other wine will do! You ain't much if you ain't Dutch.

› SERVES 8–10

OXTAILS: Start the day before you wish to serve. Wipe oxtails with damp paper towels. Season well with salt and pepper. In a large sauté pan, heat the oil over medium-high heat. Sear the oxtail pieces, a few at a time, and transfer to a large Dutch oven. Add water to cover. Bring to a boil, lower heat and simmer slowly, covered, until the meat falls off the bones (about 3½ to 4 hours). Strain meat from stock and refrigerate both, separately. The next day, remove and discard all fat, bone and gristle and cut the meat into small pieces.

BEANS: Place beans in a saucepan, cover with cold water (by 2 inches) and bring to a boil over medium-high heat. Drain. Cover beans with fresh water, bring to a boil, lower heat and simmer, covered, until beans are very soft, anywhere from 45 to 80 minutes. Drain. Push beans through a sieve and add the bean paste to the oxtail broth, along with the pieces of meat. Bring the soup to a boil, add Madeira and a pinch of cayenne and salt to taste. The soup may be thinned out to the desired texture with water. Serve hot.

NOTE Uncle Bill used Lillooet speckled beans, grown by the local First Nations people—he said they were the best!

OXTAILS
2 oxtails (about 4 lb),
    cut into 2-inch pieces
    (ask the butcher to cut)
salt and pepper, to taste
1 Tbsp vegetable oil

BEANS
1½ cups red Mexican beans or
    small red beans or Lillooet
    speckled beans (see note)
1 cup dry Madeira wine
    (called Sercial)
pinch of cayenne pepper,
    or to taste

› KELP SALAD

PING LI

I used to have potluck parties almost every week, at home in Shenyang City, in the Liaoning province of China. Friends would bring their favourite dish or a newly learned one to my house for everyone to enjoy. Five years ago, when I was still living in China, my friend Sa brought this delicious kelp salad to my potluck party. I had heard of kelp salad before but had never tried it. It was the most popular dish at the party and I fell in love with it. Sa taught me how to make her kelp salad and told me the most important step to remember is to soak the green bean vermicelli. But it should never be left too long in the hot water! And then you must keep it under running cold water for at least two minutes, to stop it cooking further. If you don't, the salad will taste soggy rather than crispy.

SALAD
35-g pkg kelp, pre-shredded
100-g pkg green bean
  vermicelli (this is a mung
  bean product)
1 medium carrot, peeled
  and julienned

SEASONING
1 tsp salt
1 tsp granulated sugar
½ clove garlic, minced
1 tsp chili oil
½ tsp white vinegar

› SERVES 6

SOAK kelp in cold water for 15 minutes, then drain and set aside. Place green bean vermicelli in a large bowl. Pour boiling water overtop and soak until soft (about 3 minutes), then drain and leave under running cold water for 2 minutes. Drain all excess water and cut into short pieces.

MIX all salad and seasoning ingredients in a big salad bowl and it's ready to serve. The ingredients listed yield about 8 cups of salad.

VANDEE'S SOM TAM

(GREEN PAPAYA SALAD)

TIMBERLY GEORGE

The first time I left home to travel was with my best friend, Lindsay. We backpacked around Malaysia, Indonesia and Thailand. After my first meal there, I fell in love with Thailand and decided I was going to become a Buddhist and live in the "land of smiles" forever. I'm not yet a Buddhist and I reside in Vancouver, but I've been back to Thailand since. Whenever people travel to Thailand I tell them they must go to Pai, and they must stay at Peter and Vandee's Hut and they must, must have Vandee's Som Tam Salad. I stayed there for over two weeks and was allowed to watch her as she cooked. Vandee would say, "Do you like *farang* (Westerner) spicy or local spicy?" I'd always say local spicy and she would just laugh, and say, "No, no, you cannot handle local spicy." The som tam, or green papaya salad, quickly became my favourite dish and each day, as I watched her make it for me, I would pay close attention to the details. Soon I had her whole recipe in my head. I now hold Thai nights for my close friends, and Lindsay comes over and retells stories of our travels. While I'm cooking away, the smile on my face is as large as those in the land of smiles all put together as I re-live the *tuk-tuk* trips, fighting with cockroaches in our sleeping quarters, moped rentals and trekking through the northern jungles.

2–3 cups grated green papaya
1 large handful fresh long green beans, chopped into 1- or 2-inch pieces, blanched tender but still crisp
8–12 cherry tomatoes or other small tomatoes, cut in half
3 cloves garlic (or as many cloves as you like!)
juice of 1 small lime
1 or more green chilies
  1 = farang (Westerner) spicy
  2 = medium spicy
  3 = hot
  4+ = Thai spicy!
¼ cup light soya sauce
1 Tbsp granulated sugar, or more to taste
¼–½ cup chopped roasted peanuts (not raw)

> SERVES 4–6

MIX grated papaya in a large bowl with green beans and tomatoes. Grind garlic, lime juice, chilies, soy sauce and sugar together using a mortar and pestle (or just crush garlic and mix well with the other intredients). Pour over the papaya mixture. Mix well. Sprinkle with peanuts and serve cold. Som tam is meant to be eaten with chopsticks. And depending on the spice level, you may need a cold beer to wash it down!

› MARINATED EGGPLANT

TINA NEALE

It was Christmas 1996 and I was travelling with three girlfriends in Morocco. Upon our arrival in Tangier, we piled into a taxi and headed south to the small coastal town of Azilal. It was pitch dark and raining heavily, and the hostel where we had planned to stay was nowhere to be found. On top of that, we appeared to be the only women out in public as we spent an hour traipsing up and down the streets in search of accommodation. We passed in front of a large café in the town square several times. It was filled entirely with men dressed in pointy-hooded *jalabas* (robes), sipping from steaming glasses of fresh mint tea and watching our plight with amusement. Finally two local boys showed us to an inexpensive hotel and later to a small restaurant furnished with white plastic patio sets. While the proprietor's wife prepared our couscous and vegetables, we were served fresh crusty bread and a delicious appetizer, which we later learned, through a series of hand gestures and mangled French phrases, was marinated eggplant. We never saw another marinated eggplant during our travels in Morocco, so it's hard to say if this is a typical Moroccan dish. Nevertheless, this meal remained the most memorable of the trip. I re-created this recipe when I returned home and I now make it for dinner parties and special occasions, where it's always a hit—and a conversation starter too!

1 large eggplant
½ cup balsamic vinegar
⅓ cup olive oil
4 cloves garlic, crushed
1 bunch fresh cilantro, chopped (about ½ cup), or to taste
1 Tbsp ground cumin
1 Tbsp chili powder
2 Tbsp chopped fresh basil
cayenne pepper, to taste

› SERVES 4 AS AN APPETIZER

PREHEAT the oven to 350°F. Cut eggplant in half lengthwise, place face down on a parchment-lined baking sheet and cover lightly with aluminum foil. Bake for about 40 to 50 minutes, or until eggplant is very soft. While eggplant is baking, combine remaining ingredients for marinade. Place eggplant cut-side up in a serving dish and scoop out seed clusters if desired. Pour marinade over top and refrigerate overnight. Before serving, remove eggplant from the refrigerator and bring to room temperature. Serve with slices of crusty baguette.

YUM SOM-O

(POMELO SALAD)

MONTRI RATTANARAJ, *Montri's Thai Restaurant*

I grew up in Thailand. My mother, grandmother and four sisters were all fabulous cooks, and I was the youngest and the only boy, so life was very good for me! My grandmother lived in the south, in a beautiful, quiet area right on the ocean. She grew her own vegetables and cooked with all the fabulous local seafood, so every meal was fresh, fresh, fresh. This salad is one of my favourites. A pomelo resembles a giant grapefruit, and like grapefruit, there are both pink and white varieties. It is now being imported into Canada from Thailand, China and the U.S. If you can't find it at your local market, you can substitute grapefruit.

> SERVES 4

PEEL the fruit with a sharp knife, taking off all the thick skin. Divide into segments by cutting between the membranes. Discard membranes, remove seeds and put the segments in a bowl.

CRUSH garlic in a separate bowl or pound with a mortar and pestle, then mix in the chili, sugar, fish sauce and lime juice, mixing well so sugar dissolves. Add dried shrimp and lemon grass and mix well. Pour over the pomelo segments and toss gently.

1 pomelo or 2 grapefruits
1 small clove garlic
1 red Thai chili, seeded and sliced (optional)
1 Tbsp sugar (preferably palm sugar)
1 Tbsp fish sauce *or* salt to taste
2 Tbsp fresh lime juice
¼ cup dried shrimp, very finely sliced
1 stem lemon grass, very finely sliced

▸ CHOLA

(CHICKPEA SALAD)

JAMALUDDIN MUHAMMAD

This is a recipe from my home in Bangladesh. The name of the dish is Chickpea Salad (*chola* in Bengali). It can be served as a side dish with meals or as a snack, and is very popular during Ramadan (the month of fasting) for breaking the fast. A lot of people at my workplace like it, so I would like to share it with others! You can omit the eggs if you are cholesterol-conscious and you can make it hot by increasing the chili powder, up to one teaspoon. If you increase the turmeric, however, it may taste bitter.

2 medium eggs
2 Tbsp olive oil or vegetable oil
½ small onion, chopped
¼ tsp turmeric
¼ tsp chili powder
½ tsp cumin
½ tsp salt
two 19-oz cans chickpeas,
    drained, rinsed and
    drained again
1 medium tomato, sliced
a few leaves of cilantro
    (optional)

▸ SERVES 6–8

PLACE eggs in a small pot of cold water. Bring to a boil and turn off heat. Let eggs sit in the hot water for 10 minutes. Heat oil in a frying pan over medium heat. Add onion and sauté, stirring for a few minutes until golden. Add turmeric, chili powder, cumin and salt. Stir for 1 minute to mix well. Add chickpeas. Cook over medium heat for a further 7 to 10 minutes until well mixed and not watery. Slice eggs and mix gently into the mixture. You can serve immediately, garnished with sliced tomatoes and fresh cilantro, or allow to cool—it tastes good hot or at room temperature.

DONG BEI LIANG CHAI

(NORTHEAST CHINESE SALAD)

MEI CAO

I grew up in Mudanjiang, a small city near Harbin, the capital city of the province of Manchuria in northeast China. It's very cold and dry there in the winter, with weather similar to that of Toronto. However, the summers are beautiful and very much like Vancouver's, and maybe that's why we immigrated here. This dish is a very popular homestyle salad from Manchuria—we don't have many other salad dishes there. When my husband took me to a restaurant called Northeast Cuisine, I fell in love with it. The owner, Mr. Wang, is a good friend of my husband's, so he was willing to share his secret recipe with me. It is not a difficult dish to make and the peanut butter is the secret to its success. Thanks to Mr. Wang, it has become my signature dish and I am always happy to serve it to others.

> SERVES 6

PLACE vermicelli in a bowl and cover with boiling water. Allow to sit for 8 to 10 minutes, stirring 2 or 3 times. Drain and rinse under cold running water for 5 minutes and drain again.

STIR-FRY pork in a hot frying pan with 4 to 5 teaspoons of oil for 30 seconds. Add soy sauce. Reduce heat to low until meat is cooked (about 1 minute).

MAKE chili oil by mixing hot oil and chili pepper. Set aside.

MIX the dressing ingredients well, adding the chili oil (you can remove the chilies if desired). Put all the vegetables in a salad bowl, with cooked pork on top. Toss the dressing with the salad when you're ready to serve.

SALAD

1 pkg green bean vermicelli (100 g)
7 oz pork, very thinly sliced or shredded
4–5 Tbsp vegetable oil
1 tsp light soy sauce
1 medium cucumber, julienned
1 medium carrot, julienned
½ medium Chinese cabbage, shredded

DRESSING

3 tsp vegetable oil, heated
2 tsp finely sliced fresh chili pepper
1½ tsp granulated sugar
1 tsp salt
2 tsp smooth peanut butter
4 tsp vegetable oil
3 tsp light soy sauce
5 tsp white vinegar
4 cloves garlic, finely chopped

› CITRUS QUINOA SALAD

LINDA ACOSTA

My husband is from Peru, and although he is not a fan of quinoa, I really love it! We have been to Peru several times and I always like to come back with a new recipe because Peruvian food is so flavourful and varied. This recipe was given to me by my husband's cousin. I love it because unlike most other grains, quinoa is a complete protein and is also rich in B vitamins, fibre and iron. Note that quinoa should be well rinsed before cooking as its natural coating has a bitter taste.

› SERVES 4–6

QUINOA: Combine the quinoa with water and salt in a saucepan. Bring to a boil on high heat. Cover, lower heat and simmer very gently for 15 minutes. If quinoa is not yet tender and the water is gone, add a further ¼ cup water and cook until quinoa is tender to the bite. If any liquid remains, remove lid, raise heat and cook, stirring, until it evaporates. Fluff quinoa with a fork and transfer to a large bowl to cool.

SALAD: In a small mixing bowl, whip oil, grated onion, chili paste and brown sugar. In another bowl, combine the orange and lime juice with the rice vinegar and citrus zest. Slowly whip the juice mixture into the oil mixture until thoroughly combined. Season with cumin, cayenne, salt and pepper. To the large bowl of quinoa, add chives, carrots, cilantro and raisins and toss to mix well. Add enough dressing to coat. Let grain absorb flavours for one hour at room temperature or refrigerate overnight.

TO SERVE, bring salad to room temperature and sprinkle with pecans, if desired.

NOTE Leftover dressing makes an excellent marinade for poultry.

QUINOA
1 cup quinoa, rinsed
½ cup water
½ tsp salt

SALAD
½ cup vegetable oil
1 Tbsp grated white onion
1 Tbsp Asian chili paste
1 Tbsp dark brown sugar
½ cup orange juice
1 Tbsp fresh lime juice
1 Tbsp combined zest of
    lemon, lime and orange
1 Tbsp rice vinegar
¼ tsp ground cumin
cayenne, salt and pepper
    to taste

2 Tbsp chopped chives
½ cup grated carrots
½ cup chopped cilantro
½ cup raisins
½ cup pecans (optional),
    toasted and roughly
    chopped

TON SHABU HIYAYAKO

(PORK JOWL SALAD)

TINN CHAN, *Gyoza King Izakaya Japanese*

My parents emigrated from Hong Kong and opened Gyoza King in 1993 as a traditional Chinese-Japanese restaurant with homemade dumplings as a specialty. At that time, most Japanese restaurants in Vancouver had only sushi on the menu. The restaurant was not doing as well as we wanted, and we had to come up with a new concept before getting to the point of no return. *Izakaya*-style restaurants are very popular in Japan with nine-to-five white-collar and blue-collar men, for hanging around after a long day of hard work. Izakaya means "neighbourhood pub" in Japanese, and they serve a tapas menu. My wife, who is Japanese, and I brought the concept of izakaya to Gyoza King and introduced Japanese tapas to Vancouver. It took us years to explain to Vancouverites that the Japanese do not eat just raw fish, and we have a slogan for our restaurant: "No Sushi!" This salad is one of our favourites.

> SERVES 2–4

IN a medium saucepan, bring 8 cups water to a boil. Drop pork jowl slices into the water and boil for about 2 minutes, or until the meat turns white. Drain and put the meat slices in a bowl of ice water. When cold, drain and pat dry. Set aside.

PLACE onion slices under cold running water for up to 15 minutes and pat dry. Prepare first dressing by combining all ingredients. Do the same to prepare the second dressing.

CUT tofu into ½-inch cubes. Toss mixed greens with tofu cubes and sliced onion and place on a big plate. Then pour on the first dressing. Place the pork jowl slices on the mixed greens. Drizzle half of the second dressing over top. To finish, sprinkle with green onion and sesame seeds. Offer more of the second dressing to those who enjoy a stronger taste.

8 cups water

5–6 oz pork jowl meat (packaged thinly sliced and found in frozen section of Chinese markets)

¼ onion, thinly sliced

1 small pkg soft tofu (300 g)

4 cups mixed greens, washed and patted dry (300 g)

chopped green onion for garnish

black sesame seeds for garnish

FIRST DRESSING

1 Tbsp soy sauce

1 Tbsp rice vinegar

2 Tbsp olive oil

½ tsp grated ginger

½ tsp grated garlic

SECOND DRESSING

1 Tbsp Korean hot bean paste

1 tsp kimchi base

½ tsp oyster sauce

1½ tsp water

❯ FASSOLAKIA

(BRAISED GREEN BEANS AND POTATOES WITH TOMATO SAUCE)

GEORGIA KAMBOLIS

I was born in Patras, which is the capital of the Achaia region and the largest city in the Peloponnese, Greece. Farmers would come to our neighbourhood with their carriages and horses and sell their freshly harvested vegetables right on the street. This was a social gathering—all the women would gather and make their purchases and discuss the news of the neighbourhood. Making fassolakia was also a social experience. My brothers and sisters and I, six of us in total, would prop ourselves up at our large family table, and then my mother would put a big basket of beans in the middle and we would clean and trim them. (My three brothers would sometimes gleefully throw the beans at my sisters and me.) We were *included* in this recipe, and I think that it taught us to understand the fun and work that went into food preparation.

2 lb fresh whole green beans
½–¾ cup olive oil, divided
1 large onion, diced
3–4 cloves garlic, finely chopped
1½ cups chopped fresh flat-leaf parsley
½–1 tsp chopped fresh chili pepper
sea salt, to taste
2 large potatoes, peeled and cut into quarters
3 cups finely chopped fresh, ripe tomatoes or canned tomatoes
pinch of granulated sugar

country bread
feta cheese

❯ SERVES 8

TRIM the ends of beans and the strings from both sides, then cut each bean in half.

TAKE half the oil and heat over medium heat in a large shallow pan. Sauté onion and garlic for about 3 minutes. Add green beans, parsley, chili pepper and salt to taste. Mix well to ensure beans are coated with the onion mixture. Season potatoes with salt and place them on top, in one layer. Pour tomatoes and the remaining oil over them.

REDUCE the heat to low, cover and simmer for about 30 to 45 minutes. Potatoes should be cooked and most of the juices absorbed. Do not stir; simply shake the pan gently to prevent sticking. Add a little water if it needs more liquid. Remove the pan from the heat and let cool for 15 minutes.

ENJOY with country bread and with pieces of feta cheese crumbled on top of the beans. Fassolakia can also be served as a side dish, with fish, lamb or veal.

> MOHINDER'S BEANS DE DAL

HEIDI SIDHU

This is my mother-in-law, Mohinder's, recipe and it's my husband, Jug's, favourite dish. Mohinder has never followed a recipe, let alone written one down. She is Indo-Canadian; I'm first-generation Canadian with a German-Hungarian background, and I very much possess a measuring mind. It was a challenge getting Mohinder to slow down so I could measure everything. The words "some" and "this much," said while holding her hands in the air, didn't translate easily, but we managed quite well! The real story behind Beans de Dal lies in our honeymoon, which was a six-month trip to India. Jug was excited to try Beans de Dal in the fatherland, and he tried and tried, but could not find it. He asked at people's homes, in restaurants and at *dabas* (small roadside shacks where mainly truckers eat), and he still couldn't find it. He was very disappointed and had pretty much resigned himself to the fact that it wasn't going to be a part of his experience. Then one day a waiter asked Jug what he wanted. The conversation carried on in Hindi and went something like, "What do you have?" and "I don't know what that is." The waiter was getting annoyed and hauled Jug over to where there were two big pots, one of which held the elusive Beans de Dal. Jug yelped with joy, hugging the waiter, who was looking more than a little scared at that point. Jug found out it was called *rajma dal* and pretty much ate it every day for the rest of the trip. His dad and everyone in the community had been here in Vancouver so long that the name of the dal had been Canadianized. It never occurred to us that the name sounded very English, and French for that matter. So the rajma dal recipe lives happily in our family in its Canadian incarnation as Beans de Dal.

3 cups dried kidney beans

TARKA
2 Tbsp butter
1 large onion, diced
11 cloves garlic, chopped
2 Tbsp chopped fresh ginger
2–3 green chilies, chopped
1 tomato, diced
2 tsp turmeric
½ tsp caraway seeds
1 tsp salt, plus more to taste

3 tsp garam masala
⅓ cup chopped cilantro
  (optional)

WASH beans. There are three different ways to prepare the dried beans:

1. A pressure cooker will cook beans in 30 minutes. Do not fill the pot more than halfway.

2. OR if you don't have a pressure cooker, place beans in a pot, cover by 2 inches with cold water, bring to a boil and drain. Put beans back into the pot and cover with fresh water, bring to a boil, then lower heat and simmer until soft, from 45 to 80 minutes.

3. OR soak beans for 4 hours or overnight, discard the water and cook beans in 5 to 6 cups fresh water until soft.

TARKA is the base ingredient in Punjabi food. To make it, melt butter in a large non-stick sauté pan. Add onion, garlic and ginger. Sauté until onion becomes translucent, stirring occasionally. Add chilies, tomato, turmeric, caraway seeds and salt and cook gently for 1 minute.

ONCE beans are cooked, drain and purée lightly with a blender to give them a slightly creamy texture. Add 3 more cups of water to the cooked bean mixture. Add the tarka, garam masala and cilanto and let simmer until heated through and slightly thickened. Add extra salt if needed. Serve over basmati rice.

➤ MAIN DISHES

BOEMBO BALI TAHOE

(TOFU WITH BALI-STYLE SAUCE)

MARGARET GALLAGHER,
CBC Radio's *The Early Edition*

This recipe is from *Atoeran Masak Vegetarisch*, a cookbook of Buddhist vegetarian recipes from Indonesia, published by my great-grandmother in Java in 1935. Our family had a very large publishing house in Indonesia, and my grandmother, Tan Po Hwa Niu, grew up with a huge household staff and never had to set foot in the kitchen. That is, she didn't until political upheaval forced her to immigrate to England in the late 1960s. At fifty-seven, my grandmother taught herself to cook using a dog-eared copy of her mother's cookbook that she'd brought from Indonesia. After my grandmother passed away, my mother, Kwee Tien Tjoe, gave me the last copy of this cookbook. The recipes are written in Bahasa Indonesian, with the old Dutch-style spellings. My grandmother has pencilled notes around her favourite recipes. My mother translated this particular recipe and recently we cooked it together for the very first time. I think our grandmothers would have approved of the results.

› SERVES 4

FLAVOUR BASE: Blend base ingredients together with a mortar and pestle or a food processor to form a coarse paste.

OTHER INGREDIENTS: Heat up oil in a frying pan and add the paste. Simmer paste over medium heat until fragrant and soft (about 5 minutes). Add coconut milk and 1 to 2 tablespoons of water. Simmer 1 to 2 minutes. Add tofu and eggs and stir gently. Cover and simmer over low heat for 15 to 20 minutes, stirring gently every 5 minutes.

SERVE over rice. You may want to sprinkle with fried onions for garnish. If you're feeling really spicy, serve it with a dollop of sambal (Indonesian chili sauce) on the side.

NOTE For a veggie-laden variation, you can add fresh green beans and/or canned bamboo shoots when you add the tofu and eggs.

FLAVOUR BASE

5–10 fresh red chilies, seeds removed (*Note* 10 chilies will make for a very, very hot sauce. Don't be ashamed if you scale back!)

6–8 cloves garlic

6 shallots, coarsely chopped

1 tsp salt

1 Tbsp granulated sugar

1 Tbsp dried cilantro

1–2 tsp tamarind paste

2–4 slices fresh, peeled galangal* (you can substitute 1–2 slices fresh ginger)

2 salah leaves* (optional)

1 candlenut* (optional, but do not use any substitutions)

2 tsp vegetable oil, for frying

OTHER INGREDIENTS

one 398-mL can coconut milk (1¾ cups)

1 lb medium-firm tofu, cut into 2-inch cubes

4 hard-cooked eggs, peeled and left whole

1 jar Indonesian-style deep-fried onions* for garnish (optional)

*Available at some Asian specialty stores

MOIRA'S SRI LANKAN CASHEW-NUT CURRY

MOIRA DE SILVA

About thirty years ago, as a young woman in Scotland, I fell madly in love with a very handsome young man from Sri Lanka. After a whirlwind courtship, during which I was wooed by spicy curries I did not like and that were quite alien compared to the bland local food I was accustomed to, I got married to my love. The day after our Scottish wedding, we flew to Sri Lanka for our honeymoon. When we arrived at my in-laws' house, I was faced with a second wedding ceremony plus a huge reception to which all the family members had been invited. As you can imagine, I was incredibly nervous. I was a foreign bride who did not know anything about the culture or the food. I remember several things about that day—the warm wishes of my husband's family, my first attempt at wearing a saree and the wondrous array of food. There was so much food that most of it is blurred in my memory. I remember the sight of a huge table with about twenty different dishes. I also remember my brand new husband's words to me on the way to his homeland: "You must always have a second and a third helping of food, otherwise people in my country will think you are rude." The only food I really remember in detail from this occasion was a fantastic buriyani, a hot onion dish and a cashew-nut curry. There were other wonderful dishes of chicken, fish, prawns, meat, vegetables and so on, but I remember them as too hot with chili for my bland Scottish taste. I remember the cashew-nut curry as it was the first time I had ever tasted cashews. It was a favourite of my father-in-law, and my mother-in-law taught me to make it. Today, many years later, this dish is a favourite at family gatherings and dinner parties, especially with my vegetarian friends. You can enjoy it with steamed rice and a salad or with spicy dishes such as lentils and vegetable curries. I would like to add that today I love to cook and eat the hot, spicy dishes that were alien to me all those years ago!

CURRY POWDER

8 tsp coriander seeds
6 tsp cumin seeds
3 tsp fennel seeds
1 tsp whole cloves
1 tsp green cardamom pods
1 tsp pepper
1 tsp mustard seeds
1 tsp ground nutmeg
1 tsp rice
one 2-inch cinnamon stick

CURRY

1 lb raw (unroasted) whole
    cashew nuts
1 large red onion, chopped
6 whole cloves
6 green cardamoms, ground
one 2-inch cinnamon stick
    (it should be true Ceylon
    cinnamon, not cassia,
    if possible)
½ tsp turmeric
3 hot green chilies, or to taste,
    chopped
¼ tsp whole fenugreek seeds
1 tsp cumin seeds, ground
salt to taste
1–2 tsp roasted curry powder
    (recipe provided)
1–2 tsp lime juice or lemon
    juice
6–10 Tbsp coconut milk, or
    more to taste, divided
water to cover (about 1–2 cups)

‹ SERVES 6–8

CURRY POWDER: In a dry heavy pan (cast iron is good) roast each curry powder ingredient individually, until the seeds turn a little darker and give off an aromatic smell, then grind and mix.

NOTE If you do not want make your own curry you can experiment by using commercially made curry powder (not the yellow variety).

CURRY: Place nuts in a bowl, cover with cold water and soak for 8 hours or overnight. Mix all ingredients except curry powder, lime juice and half the coconut milk in a large saucepan. Cover with water, using 1 to 2 cups as needed. Bring to a boil, lower heat and simmer, covered, for about 1 hour, or until nuts are soft. Add curry powder and cook for another 10 minutes. Add the remaining coconut milk and bring to a boil. Salt to taste. Add lime juice and serve.

If you can, buy the following optional ingredients from a Sri Lankan or Asian store and add them to the recipe with the turmeric, fenugreek and cumin:

2 pieces pandanus leaf, chopped into 2-inch pieces
curry leaves (about 20)

› CHICKPEA STEW

My husband and I had a memorable trip to Spain in October 2003. We enjoyed fabulous food everywhere we went from Madrid to Barcelona, including high in the Pyrenees Mountains. Our most memorable city for food was San Sebastian in the Basque region of Spain. My husband is addicted to any meal with peas, beans or lentils, so when we found a restaurant featuring a chickpea stew we knew that this was the spot for dinner. The exuberant waiter delighted us with an explanation of the ingredients, though the exact measurements and quantities were difficult to follow. But to our delight another waiter gave us the recipe in English. Each time we make this (frequently!) our memories of Spain are refreshed, remembering the quaint below-ground restaurant in the old town run by a family consisting of Grampa, two sons, one daughter, one daughter-in-law and a four-year-old granddaughter, who was so adorable with her big smile when she hid behind Daddy's legs. The following is the result, with some additions and changes made by us.

2 cups dry chickpeas
   or two 19-oz cans (5 cups)
   chickpeas, drained
3–4 Tbsp olive oil, divided
2 large onions, chopped
1 large leek, well washed
   and chopped, using white
   and light green parts
1 large ham bone or pork hock
   (doesn't have to be smoked)
2–3 cans beer, 355-mL size
salt and pepper, to taste
3–4 chorizo sausages (usually
   pre-cooked, but not always—
   ask butcher)
1 red chili, seeded and
   chopped (optional)
1 cup shredded green cabbage

› SERVES 4–6

IF using dry chickpeas, place in a saucepan and cover with cold water by 2 inches, bring to a boil and drain. Cover with fresh water, bring to a boil, lower heat, cover and simmer until barely soft (not mushy as they'll get more cooking). If using canned chickpeas, rinse chickpeas with cold water before adding to stew.

HEAT 2 tablespoons of the oil in a large pot. Sauté onion and leek until soft and translucent. Add ham bone or pork hock and 2 cans of beer. Bring to a boil, lower heat and simmer, partly covered, until meat is tender. This could take up to 2 hours.

ADD chickpeas. Cut chorizo into bite-sized pieces. If chorizo is not pre-cooked, add along with chickpeas. If chorizo is pre-cooked, add later, when the stew is almost done, just to heat it through. Slowly simmer again, uncovered, until chickpeas are tender. Add more beer if necessary to keep the stew quite moist. (But not too soupy!) Add salt and pepper, as well as the remaining oil, to taste. Add red chili if desired. Put shredded cabbage on top of the stew. Cover and keep hot until cabbage wilts, then stir cabbage into the stew.

SERVE hot in bowls with crusty Spanish bread. Rye bread is also great. More cabbage is good. All ingredients can be added or deleted as desired.

We like to serve another Spanish dish on the side, instead of a salad: Wilt spinach in a steamer. Remove to a bowl and toss with a little olive oil and sautéed garlic. Toss with browned pine nuts. Serve at room temperature or hot.

NONNA LINA'S VEGETARIAN PIZZA

ELSA FOGALE

My mother, Lina Rossi, arrived in Canada from northern Italy in 1956 with three very young children. Believe it or not, she was introduced to pizza in Canada by her new neighbour, Signora Vittoria, who had arrived from southern Italy. The recipes of northern and southern Italy are quite diverse, as are the dialects. It took my mother over a year to understand what Signora Vittoria was saying! As children, my siblings (soon there were six) and I would visit this dear soul and arrive home with thick slices of fragrant homemade pizza. My mom learned the basics of making pizza dough from Signora Vittoria and then, by trial and error, she succeeded in personalizing her own recipe. Today, my children and I feel that Nonna Lina's pizza rivals the best pizza in Italy. This pizza is enjoyed hot or cold and always disappears quickly at our very large family gatherings.

> MAKES THREE 12 × 16 INCH PIZZAS

PIZZA DOUGH: In a very large bowl, whisk together water, milk, egg, sugar, salt, yeast and 2 cups of the flour until the batter is smooth. Let the mixture rise until doubled and spongy, about 30 minutes. With a wooden spoon, gradually stir in the remaining 6 to 7 cups flour to make an elastic, slightly sticky dough. Knead the dough on a floured board for about 5 minutes. Form into a large ball. Coat the bowl used previously with 1 tablespoon oil. Place the dough in the bowl, turning to coat all surfaces with oil. Cover with wax paper (wiped with a little oil) and a tea towel. Let rise in a warm place for about 1 hour, or until dough has doubled in bulk. Punch down, then divide the dough into thirds. (At this point, one-third or two-thirds of the dough can be frozen for use another day. When you'd like to use the frozen dough, simply thaw at room temperature early in the day, then proceed as follows.)

PIZZA DOUGH

4 cups lukewarm water
½ cup lukewarm skim milk
1 egg, beaten
1 Tbsp granulated sugar
1 Tbsp salt
2 Tbsp + 1½ tsp active dry
   yeast (2½ envelopes)
8–9 cups unbleached
   flour, divided
olive oil, for greasing

TOPPING (FOR EACH PIZZA)

1 cup thick tomato sauce
1 Tbsp dried oregano
1 Tbsp chopped fresh basil
2 large cloves garlic, minced
½ cup finely chopped red onion
1 red pepper, seeded and
   chopped
¾ cup pitted, sliced black
   or green olives
1 small zucchini, coarsely
   chopped
1½ cups grated mozzarella
   cheese
½ cup grated Parmesan cheese

Or be creative and invent your
own combinations!

For each pizza, grease a 12 × 16 inch baking sheet with olive oil. Flatten the dough and press it gently onto the baking sheet until it reaches all sides and is evenly flat. Or you can roll the dough with a rolling pin on a large, lightly floured surface, then transfer it to a baking sheet.

TOPPING: For each pizza, spread tomato sauce over the dough and sprinkle all topping ingredients, except cheeses, on top. Let the pizza rise in a warm place for about 1 hour or until doubled in bulk. Preheat the oven to 375°F. Bake each pizza for 40 to 50 minutes, or until the bottom is golden.

When the pizza is almost done, remove it from the oven and sprinkle cheeses evenly on top. Return the pizza to the oven for about 5 minutes more, until cheeses melt. *Delizioso!*

HINT We use kitchen shears to cut this thick pizza.

FISH VINDAYE

DANIEL WANG

Fish Vindaye is one of my favourite dishes from home, which is Mauritius. Mauritius is a tropical island off the coast of Madagascar, on the east coast of Africa in the Indian Ocean. This fish dish, inspired by the southern Indian cuisine that came with the Indian immigrants to the island, is now forever part of the Mauritian cooking repertoire. Although the preparation is somewhat unusual (for it is neither a pickle nor a confit), the final result is well worth the wait, the meatiness of the fish contrasting beautifully with the spices. Serve at room temperature on crusty French bread—another testament to the island's colourful and varied past.

> SERVES 6

NOTE Begin this recipe one week before serving, for best results.

PREHEAT broiler. Cut tuna loin into 1-inch-thick slices. Lightly coat with oil and season with salt and pepper on both sides. Place tuna in a shallow baking dish under the broiler and cook for a total of about 5 minutes, turning once. Tuna should be just cooked through. Place in a bowl and cover to keep warm.

IN a heavy-bottomed frying pan, heat the ½ cup oil over medium-high heat. Fry turmeric for 3 to 5 minutes. Add onions, garlic and jalapeños and cook for another 5 minutes. Turn the heat off and add vinegar. Add salt to taste. Add the mustard seed and let the heat of the oil complete the cooking.

POUR the oil mixture over tuna, making sure that all of the fish is covered by the oil. Refrigerate, covered, and let rest for a week (for best results).

TO SERVE, flake the fish and drizzle some of the oil mixture over it. Cut a French baguette in half lengthwise. Arrange fish on the bottom and garnish with a few sprigs of cilantro. Slice crosswise into sandwiches. Must be served slightly chilled or at room temperature.

1½ lb tuna loin
½ cup vegetable oil, plus 1–2 tsp for tuna
salt and pepper, to taste
3 tsp turmeric
1 pkg pearl onions (about 20 onions), blanched in boiling water, peeled and root ends trimmed
6 cloves garlic, finely chopped
5 jalapeño chilies, seeded and chopped
¼ cup white vinegar
2 tsp black mustard seed
cilantro for garnish

› SEAFOOD RISOTTO

STEPHANIE BUCKINGHAM

In 1992, my husband was in the navy and was required to attend a series of meetings in Italy. So, being a Good Naval Officer's Wife, I saw it as my *duty* to go along to be supportive. We stayed in the small town of Lerici, located on the Bay of Poets. One evening, in a small beach restaurant, I had seafood risotto to die for. Speaking no Italian, I was unable to ask for the recipe. I madly wrote down what I thought were the ingredients. On my return home, I set about trying to re-create that seafood risotto. After a few trials, this is the recipe I came up with. I hope you enjoy it as much as our family does. The best thing about this recipe is that you can easily keep the ingredients on hand in case you suddenly need to entertain.

› SERVES 8–10

In a heavy pot, heat ½ cup of the oil and sauté onion over medium heat until translucent, stirring frequently. Add garlic. When garlic starts to colour, stir in 2 tablespoons of the parsley and add squid. Cook for 1 to 2 minutes or until squid turns white. Stir 2 or 3 times, then add vermouth (or white wine). When wine has bubbled for 1 minute, add tomatoes, reduce heat to low and cover the pot. Simmer for at least 45 minutes, until the oil has floated free. Don't add salt yet, as it will make the squid tough. (Risotto may be prepared to this point in advance and later reheated gently.)

In a separate pan, bring about 8 cups water to a simmer. Add rice to the squid mixture, increasing the heat to medium-high. Stir rice to coat it thoroughly. Add a ladleful of the simmering water, stirring constantly. Add another ladleful of water whenever the water has been absorbed. After 10 to 15 minutes, add salt and liberal grindings of pepper. The rice is done when it is firm but tender, without a chalky centre; the finished risotto should be just slightly runny. Add shrimp and scallops and cook them through, 2 or 3 minutes. Just before serving, take the pot off the heat and stir in the remaining 2 tablespoons oil and 1 tablespoon parsley.

½ cup + 2 Tbsp extra virgin olive oil, divided
2 onions, finely chopped
1–2 Tbsp chopped garlic
3 Tbsp chopped parsley, divided
6 oz frozen cleaned squid, chopped into ½-inch pieces
¼ cup dry vermouth *or* ½ cup white wine
one 19-oz can peeled Italian plum tomatoes, drained and chopped *or* 8 peeled fresh plum tomatoes, chopped, if very ripe ones are available
water (about 8 cups)
2 cups Italian Arborio rice
salt and pepper, to taste
1 lb cooked, peeled shrimp
1 lb scallops (leave whole if using bay scallops, cut in half if using Digby scallops)

B.C. HALIBUT CONGEE
WITH CHINESE SILVERFISH CRACKERS

ANDREW WONG, *Wild Rice*

In the house where I grew up, there was always the smell of congee simmering on the back burner. My grandmother always made it with smoked pork hock. My parents now make it with smoked turkey leg because they find it is less salty, and Dad doesn't need the extra salt. The congee houses in Chinatown serve many styles. I like the option of pork and preserved egg with fresh fried *yeow tieu* (a savoury donut usually served on the side). At the restaurant, Chef Stuart Irving is making a lighter, fresh version of this dish with a base of fish stock, B.C. halibut, cilantro and lemon. In my opinion, all congees made with care are equally delicious.

> SERVES 4

CRACKERS: Roughly chop silverfish. Combine flour, panko, water, salt, baking powder and silverfish in a medium-sized mixing bowl. Work into a fairly stiff dough. (Add a little more flour if needed.) Roll dough out on parchment paper to ⅛-inch thickness. Cut into 3 × 3 inch squares. Set aside while you make the congee.

CONGEE: Combine rice, fish stock, rice vinegar, mirin, lemon juice and zest, ginger and halibut in a heavy-bottomed pot. Heat over medium heat and cook until the mixture becomes cloudy and thickens slightly. Lower heat and adjust seasoning with salt and more lemon juice if needed. Simmer for about 40 minutes. Serve when it has the consistency of a loose, runny porridge. Just before serving, add cilantro.

WHILE the congee is cooking, fry the crackers. On another burner, heat oil until it just starts to smoke. Lay crackers in one at a time and fry on both sides until golden brown. Remove from oil to a tray lined with paper towels and season with salt.

GARNISH the congee with pea shoots, green onions and silverfish crackers (the crackers should be able to stand on end).

CRACKERS
1 lb silverfish (tiny fish found at Chinese supermarkets, either fresh or frozen)
4 cups all-purpose flour
4 cups panko (flaky Japanese breadcrumbs)
1 cup water
1 Tbsp salt, plus more for seasoning
2 Tbsp baking powder
2 cups vegetable oil for frying

CONGEE
¾ cup jasmine rice (not rinsed)
2 cups fish stock
4½ tsp rice vinegar
4½ tsp mirin (Japanese rice wine)
juice and zest of 2 lemons
1 tsp finely minced fresh ginger
1 lb halibut fillet, roughly chopped
salt, to taste
4 Tbsp finely chopped cilantro

GARNISH
1 cup pea shoots
½ cup julienned green onions

ESCOVITCHED SALMON

LOIS WOOD

We had spent the day cushioned by sand as soft as down and lulled by the sea and the sun. Then, in the evening, with high anticipation, we walked along the gravelled road to the garden restaurant where my Canadian husband was to be introduced at last to my childhood "Tuesday dinner"— escovitched kingfish. We were seated amid loops of jasmine and bougainvillea, enjoying the aromas while watching the chef and his team prepare their fare. Suddenly, the power failed throughout the town and a curtain of thick darkness fell on all of us. I recall our extreme disappointment as we contemplated the sensation of kingfish drenched in Scotch bonnet and allspice, Jamaican rice and peas, and the scrumptious dessert of fried bananas. With no electricity, dinner would be cancelled—or so we thought. As if on cue, fireflies appeared, performing what seemed like a choreographed ballet. They were swiftly followed by servers with reassuring gaslights. Next came the master chef himself, pronouncing "No problem!" After twenty years, the word "escovitched" still brings a twinkly smile to my husband's face. And well you might comment, kingfish is hard to find here. True, but "No problem!" In our Canadian-Jamaican household, the *escovitch* is always *salmon!* And this recipe has been passed on to many a friend, looking for an evening "away." Here's the secret, as told by my all-knowing Jamaican mother!

1 large fillet salmon (1½–2 lb)
1 Scotch bonnet or jalapeño chili or green pepper, sliced in rings (wear gloves if pepper is hot)
1 large onion, sliced in rings
1 medium carrot, thinly sliced
1 bay leaf
10 whole allspice berries
1 tsp salt
⅔ cup white vinegar
1¼ cups water

> SERVES 6

GRILL or barbecue salmon lightly on both sides (it should flake when tested with a fork). The general cooking rule for salmon is 8 to 10 minutes per inch of thickness, and it will continue to cook in its own heat while resting. Place salmon on a platter. Combine all other ingredients in a pot. Bring to a boil, and then lower the heat and simmer for 25 minutes. Pour this sauce over salmon and let sit for a few minutes. Serve warm, or refrigerate and serve cold.

FRICASSÉE DE LAPIN

(RABBIT STEW)

ERWIN DOEBELI, *William Tell Restaurant*

I grew up in Switzerland and my dad raised rabbits for the family's use. This recipe was originally my grandmother's, and my mother made it for special family celebrations like birthdays and christenings. While my mother made this dish, my father was in charge of making either polenta or mashed potatoes to go with it, and he took great pride in making the "side." While we children knew that the rabbits Father raised would be used for food, we each had a pet rabbit of our own and all of our pets were safe from the stewpot! Since moving to Vancouver in the 1960s, my wife, Josette, and I have kept up the tradition of serving this special recipe at our own family celebrations.

> SERVES 4

RABBIT: Turn rabbit pieces lightly in flour to coat, shaking off excess. Heat oil in a cast-iron pot and brown the meat on all sides. Add shallots, carrots, mushrooms and garlic to the pot and brown slightly. Add the seasonings. Add wine and cook for a few minutes, then add chicken broth (just enough to cover rabbit). Season to taste. Put the lid on and simmer over low heat for 45 to 60 minutes, or until meat can be easily pierced with a knife. Do not overcook. Remove the rabbit pieces and arrange on a serving dish. Taste the sauce, adjust the seasoning and pour it over the rabbit. Serve immediately.

POLENTA: Blend cornmeal and 1½ cups of the water into a smooth mixture. Bring remaining water and bouillon cube to a boil in a large heavy saucepan. Gradually stir in the cornmeal mixture. (If using vegetable stock, mix with cornmeal and bring to a boil.) Cook over low heat, stirring frequently, until thick and smooth (about 20 minutes). Beat in butter and cheese and salt to taste. Serve with the rabbit.

NOTE The leftover polenta is very good in the morning with fried eggs. Cut it into pieces and fry it in a little butter and vegetable oil.

RABBIT

1 rabbit, about 3 lb, cut into pieces
flour for dredging
3 Tbsp + 1½ tsp olive oil
10 medium shallots, peeled
3 medium carrots, peeled and cut into 2-inch pieces
3 oz medium-sized brown mushrooms, cut in half
3 cloves garlic
4 sprigs fresh thyme
1 bay leaf
salt and pepper, to taste
1 cup dry white wine
1 cup chicken broth

POLENTA

1½ cups cornmeal
4½ cups water, divided
1 vegetable bouillon cube *or* use vegetable stock instead of water and omit the bouillon cube
1 Tbsp butter
½ cup grated Swiss Gruyère cheese
salt, to taste

ANITROTTO MAMMA DELIA

(BREAST OF DUCK MAMMA DELIA)

UMBERTO MENGHI, *Circolo Restaurant*

This recipe brings back memories of growing up in Casa Menghi. Mamma Delia made this duck breast for special occasions, like my first communion, or weddings, Easter and Christmas. To young kids it tasted crispy and crunchy. Mmmm … *molto buono!*

> SERVES 2

2 medium duck breasts
salt and pepper, to taste
1 Tbsp olive oil
1 large egg, beaten
½ cup breadcrumbs
1 Tbsp dried lavender, to sprinkle over the finished dish

PREHEAT the oven to 475°F. Make two small incisions on the skin side of each breast. Salt and pepper the breasts to taste. Heat oil in a saucepan over medium heat. Place duck breasts in the pan skin-side down. Fry for 3 to 4 minutes per side. Remove duck from the pan and dry thoroughly with paper towels.

PLACE beaten egg and breadcrumbs in separate flat bowls. Dip each breast first in egg then in breadcrumbs. Place breasts skin-side up in a baking dish and roast for 20 minutes. The duck is done when the meat offers some resistance when pressed but still has some give to it. The duck breasts are best when cooked until slightly pink in the middle.

SPRINKLE with lavender and serve with fresh seasonal vegetables. *Buon appetito!*

➤ PAPA JACOB'S POULET FARCI

MICHEL JACOB, *Le Crocodile Restaurant*

My father always wanted to become a chef. However, when he was the age to start an apprenticeship, World War II interfered. After the war there were very few restaurants in France and he had little opportunity to realize his dream. Growing up, I enjoyed watching him cook at home every Sunday. He would prepare wonderful veal roasts stuffed with sweetbreads, whole fish and this delicious chicken, among other dishes, but never the vegetables or any part of the meal except for the main dish. He took a great interest in my career and was most proud when I became a chef—his dream realized at last.

➤ SERVES 4–5

PREHEAT the oven to 400°F. Wash chicken and dry with paper towels.

MIX ground meats with the rest of the the stuffing ingredients. Spoon into cavity of chicken without packing. Rub chicken all over with oil, salt and pepper. Skewer cavity or sew closed with kitchen string. Truss chicken and place in a shallow roasting pan. Surround with onion, carrot, leek, garlic, bay leaf and thyme. Roast 1 hour. If the skin is browning too quickly, cover it loosely with foil but do not reduce the oven temperature. Chicken is cooked when a thick part such as the thigh is pricked with a fork and the juices run clear, not pink. Remove chicken to a platter to rest.

PLACE the roasting pan over medium-high heat and stir in wine and water, scraping up the brown bits from the bottom. Reduce sauce by half and strain. Use the vegetables as garnish—they will be overcooked and delicious. After removing visible fat from the top of the sauce, pass the sauce at the table. Serve the chicken with a starch of your choice and a selection of steamed fresh vegetables.

STUFFING (FARCE)

10 oz fresh ground pork
6 oz fresh ground veal
¾ cup breadcrumbs
2 shallots, finely chopped
1 clove garlic, finely chopped
1 large egg, beaten
1 Tbsp cognac or brandy
¼ cup finely chopped fresh parsley
1 Tbsp fresh thyme leaves
1 tsp salt
several grinds pepper

CHICKEN AND VEGETABLES

one 4-lb free-range chicken
1–2 Tbsp olive oil
salt and pepper
1 large onion, cut into 6 wedges
1 large carrot, cut into 1-inch lengths
1 leek, white and light green parts, well washed, cut into 2-inch lengths
2 cloves garlic, crushed
1 bay leaf
3 sprigs fresh thyme

SAUCE

1 cup dry white wine
1 cup water

› COQ AU VIN

JOHN BLAKELEY, *Pastis Restaurant*

I grew up in France, and my first high-end professional restaurant job, when I was in my late teens,
was with a chef named Monsieur Nouvet. He was in his sixties by
that time, and his passion and love for cooking was very inspirational.
Cooking was his life, and he lived huge! He was an eccentric character,
but we respected him deeply because he was such an accomplished
chef and he treated us with respect—not a common thing for restaurant staff in France. As a mentor, he opened my eyes to the wonderful
possibilities of a culinary career. He had many secret sauces and pastry
recipes that the rest of the staff could never make as well as him, but
he shared his own home-cooking by making special lunches just for
us, when we all sat down together to eat at 11:30 before we opened
for the public. He would tell us stories about his life and the food, and
I learned so much from him. I even learned how to drink red wine at
that table—he always had a glass in his hand from eight A.M. onwards!

› SERVES 6–8

PLACE chicken and marinade ingredients in a glass or stainless-steel
bowl. Toss, cover and let sit overnight in the refrigerator.

TAKE chicken out of the marinade. Strain marinade and discard solids.
Heat oil in a heavy-bottomed pot. Pat chicken dry, season and brown
pieces. Remove chicken, drain fat and add marinade and wine vinegar to deglaze the bottom of the pot. Simmer until reduced by half.
Return chicken to the pot along with pearl onions, mushrooms and
bouquet garni, cover with beef broth and bring to a simmer. Cook
over low heat for about 30 minutes, or until chicken is done. Remove
chicken, pearl onions and mushrooms from the liquid, cover to keep
warm and set aside. Reduce cooking liquid. Combine beurre manié
ingredients well and stir into reduced liquid until thickened. Add
bacon. Adjust seasoning. Serve chicken on hot buttered egg noodles,
garnish with pearl onions and mushrooms and cover with the sauce.

CHICKEN AND MARINADE

4 lb chicken pieces
2 cups full-bodied dry red wine
1 clove garlic, crushed
1 onion, sliced
1 carrot, peeled and sliced
1 bay leaf
3 sprigs fresh thyme
4 strips bacon, coarsely
   chopped

salt and pepper
2 Tbsp vegetable oil
1 tsp red wine vinegar
2 cups pearl onions, peeled
2 cups small cremini
   mushrooms
1 bouquet garni: 1 bay leaf,
   3 parsley stalks and 3 sprigs
   fresh thyme, tied together
4 cups beef broth

BEURRE MANIÉ

1 Tbsp butter
1 Tbsp flour

1 cup diced cooked lean bacon
   (¼-inch pieces)

TURKEY WITH STICKY RICE STUFFING

GIGI SUK-YEE WONG

My family is from Guangdong province Kaiping, and I grew up in Guangzhou. We moved to Hong Kong when I was only nine years old, and I started to cook and take care of my family then. I learned basic Chinese cooking techniques from a neighbour. It wasn't until many years later that I took lessons from the cooking master Tam Kwok-mui and started to appreciate the wonderful joy of cooking. Being an actress in Hong Kong for more than twenty years, I had the chance to learn from and talk to many expert chefs and experienced cooking masters. I began to develop my own recipes and transformed myself from an actress into a writer of cookbooks. The first time I had turkey was when I went to Newcastle in England for a meeting. To be honest, it wasn't a great experience! It was very dry and salty, and it tasted like beef jerky. I didn't have turkey again for almost ten years, until I was invited to a Christmas dinner in Victoria. I was asked to make turkey for everyone. I was a bit frustrated at first, not knowing how to cook a turkey, but then I accepted the challenge and began my quest. I learned from many chefs that the secret to making a great turkey is the roasting time—twelve minutes per pound. I also tried interesting ingredients for the stuffing. Sticky rice is easy to find and it is ready to use, so I gave it a try. I was amazed by the result, and the rest is history.

TURKEY AND MARINADE
one 10-lb turkey
3 Tbsp five-spice powder
3 Tbsp oyster sauce
½ cup chicken broth *or* 2 Tbsp poultry seasoning
3 Tbsp dark soy sauce
3 Tbsp brandy
1 tsp granulated sugar
1 tsp salt

STUFFING
2 pkgs pre-cooked sticky rice (5 to 6 cups), unwrapped and mashed (available at Chinese supermarkets)

SAUCE
½ cup water
½ cup red wine
1 tsp granulated sugar

› SERVES 12 OR MORE

TURKEY AND MARINADE: Wash turkey inside and out and dry with paper towels. Mix marinade ingredients and rub all over the inside and outside of turkey. Marinate, loosely covered and refrigerated, for at least 6 hours.

PREHEAT the oven to 450°F.

STUFFING: Stuff turkey with sticky rice. Do not pack stuffing. Close the vent with skewers and kitchen string. Wrap the wing tips and the ends of the drumsticks in foil. Place turkey in a roasting pan, breast up, and put in the oven for 15 minutes, or until it turns golden.

PLACE foil over turkey, turn the heat down to 350°F and roast for 1 hour and 45 minutes. The turkey is cooked when the stuffing and mid-thigh meat have reached 165°F. Remove turkey to a platter, leaving the foil draped over top, and let rest for 20 minutes.

SAUCE: Place the roasting pan over medium heat, add water and stir up the browned bits from the bottom of the pan. Spoon off visible fat. Pour the juices from the roasting pan into a saucepan, then add red wine and sugar. Stir and cook over medium-high heat. Boil for about 5 minutes, until the sauce reduces a little. Uncover the turkey and pour the sauce into a small bowl. Carve the turkey and pass the sauce at the table.

> YELLOW CHICKEN

RACHEL NEWTON

My family background is Burmese-Chinese (Burma is the present-day Myanmar). I was born in Australia, but each of my parents emigrated with my grandparents from Burma to Australia when the Socialist government took over in Burma during the 1960s. This Burmese curry recipe has been passed from both of my grandmothers to my mother and then to my sister and me. I know there is a correct Burmese name for this dish, but we call it Yellow Chicken as the turmeric makes the chicken turn yellow.

This was my comfort food when I was growing up and I think we had it almost every week. When we were little, my sister and I would sit on the floor of the kitchen together and take turns mincing the ginger and garlic with a heavy stone mortar and pestle. The first time I travelled to Europe in my late teens, I was in Italy for six weeks on a scholarship. After a month of pasta, I called home one night and requested that my first meal when I arrived home be Yellow Chicken. Sure enough, my mother prepared it for me when I finally arrived back home. Yellow Chicken was also one of the first meals I learned to cook, and when I moved away from home, it was the favourite of my then short repertoire of ten recipes. Since leaving Australia in the early 1990s, I have travelled throughout parts of Asia and Europe and have cooked Yellow Chicken for friends I have met in various cities. Now, I live in Vancouver and I have introduced many of my Canadian friends to this dish as well.

When I first met the man who is now my husband, he did not care for curries or anything spicy, being from Winnipeg, but when I made Yellow Chicken for him, he decided he did like curries after all. My family is still in Australia, but when we see each other, my mother cooks Yellow Chicken and the memories of my childhood come flooding back. For some reason, it always tastes better when my mother cooks it for me.

2 Tbsp sunflower
  or vegetable oil
1 small yellow onion, diced
2 tsp minced garlic
1 tsp minced fresh ginger
2 tsp paprika (sweet or hot
  depending on taste)
1 tsp turmeric
1 whole chicken, cut into
  8 pieces
1–2 Tbsp mushroom soy sauce,
  to taste
1 cup chicken stock, plus
  1 extra cup chicken stock
  to use if necessary
1 cup canned tomatoes,
  with juice, diced

HEAT oil over low to medium heat in a large pot. Add onion, garlic and ginger and sauté, stirring occasionally, until golden. Add paprika and turmeric and mix into a paste (careful, it will stain clothes). Add chicken pieces and raise the heat to brown chicken. Stir to cover all pieces with the paste. Add soy sauce and chicken stock, stir well and bring to a boil. Reduce heat to medium and add tomatoes with juice. Cover and simmer for 20 minutes, stirring occasionally. Add more chicken stock if necessary. Remove cooked chicken pieces to a platter. The meat should pierce easily with a fork and the juices run clear yellow, not pink. Remove the lid, increase heat and reduce the liquid to a sauce consistency. Stir occasionally. Put chicken pieces back into the finished sauce and heat through to serve. Serve with white jasmine or basmati rice and stir-fried vegetables.

› FESINJAN

(IRANIAN WALNUT CHICKEN WITH RICE)

ROXIE GILES

Back in the 1970s, my husband, Don, and I had the good fortune to live and work in northern Iran; he in the building of a pulp mill and I in the school for children of expatriates working on the project. With an overfilled work week and many long hours on a company bus to the work site, we were thrilled to have an Iranian housekeeper. In addition to the weekly cleaning and ironing (mountains of cotton clothing), Sari would leave us a delicious "taste of Iran." In the twenty-five years since we left Iran, I have shared this meal many times. Each time I make it I remember the fine times and friendships we enjoyed overseas.

› SERVES 4

SAUCE: Heat butter in a large pan. Fry onion, stirring often, until browned. Add tomato paste and walnuts and sauté for a few minutes, stirring constantly. Add water, cinnamon, sugar, lemon juice and pomegranate juice. Cover and let cook over low heat for about 35 minutes. Taste the sauce and if you find it a bit too sour, add more sugar.

CHICKEN: Meanwhile, sprinkle chicken with poultry seasoning, salt and pepper. In a separate pan, sauté chicken in oil until browned on all sides. Set chicken aside, covered, and keep warm until the sauce is ready. Put the sautéed chicken in the sauce and let simmer a further 30 minutes.

BASMATI RICE: Basmati rice is cooked to perfection in Iran. Here's how I learned to cook it. Soak rice in room-temperature water for an hour (or more). Drain. Put rice into a large pot of boiling water (pinch of salt optional); let boil for 5 minutes. Drain. In a separate large pot, melt butter over low heat. Add rice to butter. Cover rice with a tea towel, put on the lid and cook at lowest possible heat at least 45 minutes. Turn this rice upside down on a platter. The result is beautifully cooked rice with a golden brown, crunchy top. Serve Fesinjan on top.

SAUCE

1 Tbsp unsalted butter
1 large onion, finely chopped
2 tsp tomato paste
2 cups walnuts, finely chopped
   (a food processor is ideal
   for this)
3 cups water
½ tsp cinnamon
1 tsp granulated sugar,
   plus more to taste
2 Tbsp lemon juice
1 cup pomegranate juice
   (available in any Middle
   Eastern food store)

CHICKEN

1 chicken, cut into pieces
   or 4 chicken breasts, bone in
1½ tsp poultry seasoning
1 tsp salt
pinch of pepper
2 Tbsp olive oil

BASMATI RICE

2½ cups basmati rice
pinch of salt (optional)
4 Tbsp unsalted butter

SHAWARMA DAJAAJ

(CHICKEN PITAS)

STUART MacRITCHIE

My wife and I lived for nine years in Riyadh, Saudi Arabia, where my wife taught at the Saudi Arabian International School, Riyadh (SAISR), American Section. Although the majority of children were of North American expat origin, the school was very multicultural, and as part of the multicultural exchange activities my wife took a cooking class that included this recipe. The basic recipe was handed out in typed format but as the class proceeded my wife made handwritten notes. The recipe calls for de-boned chicken; however, when we looked closely at the handwritten notes, we noticed that she had written de-boned *children!* How is that for a Freudian slip!

> SERVES 8–10

CHICKEN AND MARINADE: In a glass or stainless-steel bowl, mix together all ingredients and marinate chicken, covered, for 5 to 6 hours in the refrigerator.

ADD minced garlic to mayonnaise, to taste, and refrigerate for a couple of hours to allow the flavours to blend. Make garlic mayonnaise as you need it because garlic in oil goes bad easily.

PREHEAT the oven to 450°F. Shake excess marinade off chicken. Place chicken in a shallow roasting pan in a single layer and bake until the pieces are lightly browned, about 10 minutes. Turn once and bake until other sides are browned. Chicken is cooked when the juices run clear (not pink) if pieces are pricked with a fork. Remove from the oven, cut into thin slices, return to the pan with drippings and mix well. (For lower fat content remove the skin before slicing.)

SERVE chicken wrapped in pitas, each spread with garlic mayonnaise, some shredded lettuce, a slice of dill pickle, a French fry and lots of hot pepper sauce.

CHICKEN AND MARINADE
two 3-lb chickens, de-boned
   or boneless chicken breasts
   and thighs with skin
1 tsp salt
1 tsp pepper
1 tsp cinnamon
1 tsp ground cloves
½ tsp cayenne pepper
4 tsp ground cardamom
½ cup lemon juice

GARNISH
mayonnaise, to taste
minced garlic, to taste
8–10 pieces pita bread
8–10 lettuce leaves, shredded
8–10 dill pickle slices
8–10 hot French fries
hot red pepper sauce, to taste

ZERESHK POLO

ENSIEH RASTEGAR

Zereshk polo is an Iranian dish with rice and chicken, and ingredients such as pistachios, almonds, orange peel, carrots, zereshk (tart dried barberries), raisins and saffron. It's a luxurious and delicious food. My grandmother, who was a great cook, made it with the best possible taste and I had enjoyed this dish—before this story happened. When I was a child I used to have a chicken as a pet. I bought one or two chicks every summer and looked after them until they grew up. Most of the time they were roosters, but when I was in preschool I had a hen. Her feathers were like hana (henna) so I called her Miss Henna, Hana Khanoum. Every day when I got home from school, I went to the yard and played with her. Moreover, I loved to find her eggs, but unfortunately she did not lay any for some months, and my grandmother said that she had grown old. One day, when I went to the yard as usual, I could not find my hen, so I went to my grandmother's kitchen and told her. She looked at me with a big smile and picked up the lid of a pot that was boiling on the stove. It had a very good smell and I was hungry, but when I looked in I suddenly found out it was my chicken boiling in the pot. It was an awful feeling. I am now thirty-five, but sometimes when I eat zereshk polo I feel sick!

> SERVES 8

CHICKEN: Wipe chicken pieces clean with paper towels. Season all over with salt. Place chicken in a large sauté pan that has a lid. Add chopped onions, carrots and garlic, cover and heat over high heat. After 1 minute, lower the heat and allow chicken to cook for 30 minutes. Test for doneness and cook longer if necessary. Add saffron and heat for another 2 minutes.

CHICKEN
4 chicken breasts or thighs, bone in
salt, to taste
2 medium white onions, chopped
2 medium carrots, cut into ¼-inch dice
2 cloves garlic, finely chopped
½ tsp saffron

GARNISH
2 Tbsp julienned almonds
1 cup julienned carrots
3 Tbsp granulated sugar, divided
2 Tbsp finely julienned orange peel
1 cup zereshk (Iranian dried barberries)
4 Tbsp butter, divided
½ tsp saffron
½ cup small raisins
cooked rice (enough for 8)
2 Tbsp julienned pistachios

GARNISH: Soak the almonds in cold water for 30 minutes to soften. Drain and pat dry. Simmer carrots in a small amount of water and 1 teaspoon of the sugar until tender. Boil orange peel in water, just covered, and 1 teaspoon of the sugar until tender. Wash zereshk in a strainer, drain and pat dry. Melt 3 tablespoons of the butter in a sauté pan over medium heat and add zereshk. Cook about 1 minute. Stir in the remaining 1 teaspoon sugar and ½ teaspoon saffron and turn off the heat. Soak raisins in cold water for 15 minutes, drain, pat dry and sauté them briefly in the remaining 1 tablespoon butter, until softened.

TO SERVE, layer rice on a large platter and artistically arrange the garnish ingredients on top. You can add the chicken or serve it separately. Sprinkle the almonds and pistachios over the entire dish.

KEEMA MATAR

(SPICED GROUND MEAT WITH RAITA)

PRIYA RAMU, CBC Radio's *On the Coast*

This is by far one of my favourite comfort foods. It's called Keema Matar—it's a ground meat dish, wonderfully spiced and scrumptiously yummy. It is what I make when I get home after travelling—when I need home cooking to counter the effects of too much restaurant food or room service. I also make it on weekends because it freezes really well and is great for leftover lunches. As with most Indian food, freezing it and then reheating only makes it taste better, as the flavours intensify! In its original form, and as it was made for me growing up, Keema Matar was made with ground beef or lamb. In the interest of lower fat, I now use ground turkey or chicken, which is just as good. I eat it with raita and brown rice, Indian pickles and pappadum. Enjoy!

> SERVES 4

KEEMA MATAR: Heat oil over medium heat and fry onion until translucent and browning (about 10 minutes), stirring occasionally. Add meat and brown, breaking up lumps with a wooden spoon. Add garlic and hot pepper flakes or paprika, then coriander seed, turmeric, cumin, garam masala and ginger. Mix and fry over medium heat. Add 1 to 2 tablespoons water to prevent sticking and burning. Cook together about 5 minutes. Add tomatoes, peas, spinach, salt and water. Cover and simmer for 15 to 20 minutes. Serve with rice or chappatis and raita.

RAITA: Mix together all ingredients. Sprinkle with cumin. Serve as a side dish with rice.

KEEMA MATAR

2 Tbsp vegetable oil
1 onion, chopped
1 lb ground turkey or chicken
4 cloves garlic, finely chopped
½ tsp hot red pepper flakes *or* 1 tsp paprika
1 Tbsp ground coriander seeds
½ tsp ground turmeric
1 Tbsp ground cumin, plus a little for garnish
1 Tbsp garam masala
1 Tbsp grated fresh ginger
2 tomatoes, chopped
1 cup green peas, frozen
1 cup spinach, frozen
salt, to taste
½ cup boiling water

RAITA

1½ cups plain yogurt
½ cup chopped tomatoes
½ cup grated cucumber
¼ cup grated onion
1–2 fresh green chilies, chopped (keep the seeds if you like heat, but remove them if you don't)
¼ cup chopped cilantro
salt, to taste

COUSCOUS MARRAKESH

BILL PATON

When I was eleven in 1976–77, my parents, Jean and Doug, my two brothers, Jamie and Andy, and I (and one grandmother, for two months) travelled across Europe, North Africa and Turkish Asia for thirteen months in an orange VW van. The van was our transport, kitchen and bedroom. We had many memorable meals, but our favourite dish was Couscous Marrakesh, which my mother still makes for special occasions. It always makes us think of what we all call "the trip," which forever changed all of our lives.

> SERVES 8–10

STEW: Heat oil in a large frying pan. Sauté onion until soft with spices, including the 1 tablespoon salt. With a slotted spoon, remove onion to a large pot. In the same oil, brown lamb. Add lamb and water to onion in the large pot. Bring to a boil, lower heat and simmer 30 minutes. Add chicken and simmer 30 minutes. Add vegetables and remaining ingredients. Cook 15 minutes, or until carrots are tender. Serve on cooked couscous.

COUSCOUS: Combine water, salt and butter in a small saucepan and bring to a boil. Remove from heat and add couscous. Stir and let stand, covered, 1 minute. Return pan to low heat and stir for 3 to 4 minutes. This method allows butter to coat each grain so that they will be separate and not clump. (Or cook as label directs.)

STEW

¼ cup peanut or vegetable oil
1 cup chopped onion
1 tsp ground coriander seeds
1 tsp cayenne pepper
½ tsp saffron
1 tsp ground cumin
1 Tbsp salt
2½ lb lamb, cut into 2-inch chunks
8 cups water
one 3-lb chicken, cut up
1 lb carrots, peeled and cut into 1-inch chunks
2 green peppers, cut into ½-inch strips
4 large tomatoes, cut into wedges, or one 14-oz can tomatoes, with some of the juice drained off
1 lb squash or pumpkin, peeled and cut into 2-inch chunks
2 cups frozen peas or cut green beans
one 19-oz can chickpeas, well drained and rinsed
1 cup raisins
salt and pepper, to taste

COUSCOUS

2 cups water
1 tsp salt
2 Tbsp butter
2½ cups couscous

› CURRIED MINCED BEEF

AND FRIED CURRIED TOMATOES

RICK CLUFF, CBC Radio's *The Early Edition*

These family recipes were passed down from my mom and dad. Nothing was ever written down—each dish was just one of those things you threw together on a moment's notice, and it always tasted great. My dad, Harold, loved spicy food, and I was happy to inherit that love from him. My mom, Dorothy, had a more tender tummy (or so she thought) and always tried to cut back on the amount of curry. But whenever her back was turned, Dad would sneak into the kitchen and add more. The conversation at dinner would always turn to the spiciness of either dish, with Mom saying, "See, I told you it didn't need any more than that." Dad would smile and agree that she was right again.

> › SERVES 4

CURRIED MINCED BEEF: Heat oil or butter in a large frying pan over medium heat. Sauté onion until just soft. Add beef and brown lightly, breaking up lumps. Pour off the excess fat.

COMBINE flour with water and mix until smooth. Add curry and mix well. Add the liquid mixture to the beef and let simmer. It will form a smooth gravylike sauce. This is when you can adjust the heat of the curry to your taste, and add Louisiana Hot Sauce if you're so inclined. Serve over smooth whipped potatoes. Garnish with finely chopped green onions. Quick and easy … and delicious.

FRIED CURRIED TOMATOES: Melt 2 teaspoons butter in the bottom of a non-stick frying pan. Add thickly sliced tomatoes. Place a small dollop of butter on each tomato slice. Season with salt and pepper and as much curry as you can handle. Cook over medium heat. Carefully turn tomatoes and repeat the seasoning. Remove from heat when tomatoes are soft and delectable, and while they still retain their shape. Serve with rice, a fresh garden salad and crusty bread with chilled butter. A glass of hearty red wine is also nice.

This is a disarmingly simple recipe … but one that can be several layers deep in flavour.

1–2 Tbsp vegetable oil or butter (butter is best)
1 large onion, diced
1 lb lean minced beef
1 Tbsp all-purpose flour
1½ cups cold water
1–2 Tbsp curry, to taste (I usually use fine Madras curry)
1–2 dashes Louisiana Hot Sauce (optional!)
green onions, finely chopped for garnish

FRIED CURRIED TOMATOES
butter, about 1 Tbsp per tomato
1 tomato per person, thickly sliced (at least ½ inch)
salt and pepper to taste
curry, to taste (a strong Madras curry is my favourite)

SWEDISH TJÄLKNÖL
(LONG-ROASTED STEAK)

LENA NORMÉN-YOUNGER

In central and northern Sweden, freezers are full of moose meat because of the annual October hunt. Tjälknöl is a modern moose meat dish, invented by mistake in the era before the microwave was introduced. This somewhat odd cooking method leaves the moose steak with a lot of juice and aroma. The name derives from the two words *tjäle*, which means "frost-frozen" and *knöl*, which means "bump," thus describing a bump of meat coming out from a frozen state. The dish originated with an absentminded lady, who put a frozen moose steak in the oven on low heat to thaw and completely forgot it until the day after. By that time the steak was completely cooked. To salvage the flavour of the meat, she brined it in saltwater and added some spices. She then cut it thinly and was amazed by the tender and juicy quality of the moose meat, which normally becomes very dry in the oven. This cooking method suits not only moose meat but also other frozen cuts of beef such as the shoulder or the outer thigh. Adventurous people will even try this with frozen pieces of ostrich. Over the last 30 years, Tjälknöl has become a much-loved Swedish dish.

2¼–2½ lb moose or beef steak, frozen

3 Tbsp salt
1 Tbsp sugar
2 cups water
1 Tbsp herbs: fresh or dried basil, tarragon, rosemary and/or thyme

> SERVES 6

PREHEAT the oven to 175°F. Place the meat on a rack in a deep roasting pan so that the juices do not drip to the bottom of the oven. The duration of cooking is about 6.5 hours for each 2 pounds of meat, or when the internal part of the meat registers 160°F.

MIX the salt, sugar, water and herbs in a bowl and add the warm steak. Let the steak brine in the marinade for about 5 hours in the refrigerator. Turn the steak once an hour during the brining.

TO SERVE, take the cooled, brined meat out of the marinade and pat it dry. Cut the meat in thin slices (¼ inch) with a very sharp knife and serve it cold with a cold potato salad or a warm potato gratin.

TOURTIÈRE

NANCY JEFFERSON

When the children were very young, we started a tradition of close families gathering at our home for an early get-together and carol singing on Christmas Eve. This tradition continued for over thirty years and the numbers grew from two or three families to many more. The menu also changed with the numbers. There was, however, one item that was always on the menu—tourtière. It was the perfect dish for a group from ten to eighty, and it appealed to three generations. As the children's musical talents emerged, the evening also included a small orchestra performing the carols. Later, children became couples and a fourth generation joined the gathering. It became so big that after about thirty years, it has scaled back to being just a family gathering, but the menu still has tourtière—the grandchildren insist on it!

shortcrust pastry for
   2 covered pies

2 medium potatoes, peeled
   and chopped
1 Tbsp vegetable oil
1 lb ground pork
2 medium onions, chopped
1 lb lean ground beef
2 cloves garlic, finely chopped
1 tsp dried thyme
1 tsp dried sage
¼ tsp ground cloves
½ tsp dry mustard
1 tsp salt

> MAKES TWO 8-INCH PIES

BOIL potatoes in water to cover until very tender. Save 1 cup of the potato water and drain the potatoes. Mash potatoes and set aside. Heat a large frying pan over medium-high heat. Add oil and pork, breaking up lumps as the cooking begins. After about 10 minutes, add onions and cook until they begin to get soft. Add beef and brown slightly, again breaking up the meat as finely as possible. Add garlic, reserved potato water and all the seasonings. Simmer about 20 minutes, or until the liquid is absorbed into the mixture. Add mashed potatoes. Cool.

WHILE the mixture cools, roll pastry and fit it into the pie pans.

PREHEAT the oven to 350°F. Divide meat mixture between the 2 pies. Place top crusts on, sealing the edges. Cut a few slits in the pastry tops. Bake 40 minutes. Serve with a spicy tomato sauce or a mild salsa.

NOTE Pies may be made ahead and frozen *uncooked*. Thaw in refrigerator and bake when needed.

FRIKADELLER

(DANISH MEATBALLS)

ALESSANDRA QUAGLIA, *Provence Restaurants*

My grandmother, "Mormor," always said, "Mix some patience, some planning, some luck, some imagination, some understanding and lots of love and some good will come of it. You can have a little at the table or you can have a lot, it's not important, as long as you enjoy your time together." These words always ring loudly in my mind and heart whenever I make Danish meatballs.

> SERVES 4

MIX meat, flour, egg, onion and breadcrumbs and season to taste. Add milk slowly until combined. Add just enough to give you a thick, creamy consistency. Heat a little butter in a frying pan over medium heat. Form the meatballs with a spoon and the palm of your hand and place directly into the pan. Turn the meatballs periodically until evenly browned on all sides and cooked all the way through. Keep warm in the oven until ready to serve.

THESE meatballs are traditionally served with marinated red cabbage and/or cucumber salad, a little gravy and some boiled baby new potatoes.

1¼ lb ground pork (the better the meat, the better the frikadeller!) *or* half pork and half beef
2 Tbsp flour
1 large egg, lightly beaten
1 small onion, minced
2–3 Tbsp dry breadcrumbs
salt and pepper, to taste
¾ cup milk
butter for frying

BULGOGI

(KOREAN BBQ BEEF)

ANGIE LEE

Bulgogi is one of the most popular Korean foods, with both Koreans and foreigners. In Korean, *bul* means "fire" and *gogi* means "meat," so this is a main dish of sliced meat seasoned with spices. When I was young, I used to get very excited whenever my mom made this dish. Bulgogi was the most wonderful thing that I had ever smelled. Then, when I saw it, my mouth watered. It looked so nice with the harmony of beef and vegetables, and the taste was beyond description! This dish is ideal if grilled over smoked wood, but it's just as good made in a frying pan.

› SERVES 6–8

2½ lb rib-eye beef or sirloin, thinly sliced (about ⅓ inch)
1 Tbsp honey
1 Tbsp granulated sugar, divided
2 Tbsp soy sauce
2 tsp sesame oil
2 tsp crushed garlic, minced
1 Tbsp soju (Korean whiskey)
pinch of pepper
½ cup water
½ kiwi or ripe pear, peeled and juiced in a blender

TRIM the fat off the beef and lay meat out on a large plate. Spread honey thinly on each piece. Sprinkle a little of the sugar evenly on each piece. Allow beef to sit for 10 minutes.

IN a bowl, mix together soy sauce, sesame oil, garlic, the remaining sugar, soju, pepper and water. Set aside.

MASSAGE beef with kiwi juice using your hands. (The kiwi works as a tenderizer.) Add beef to the soy sauce mixture and mix. Allow beef to marinate for 4 hours, covered, in the refrigerator. (Thinner slices of beef can take less time.)

DRAIN marinade from meat. Preheat grill or frying pan over high heat. Cook slices until brown, 1 or 2 minutes per side. Be careful not to overcook, the meat is thin!

CORNED BEEF AND CABBAGE

TRIONA BENVIN

I grew up in Ireland in the 1970s. St. Patrick's Day is our national holiday and it always rained. My three sisters and I would trudge into town to see the parade marching through Shop Street and around Eyre Square. Our one TV station, RTE, played movies about sweet nuns in missions, sweltering beneath their habits and helping some swarthy doctor heal the sick in the jungle. The pubs were all on Sunday time and opened at seven in the evening and closed at ten. I moved to Vancouver in 1997 and met my Canadian husband here. One of my earliest successes with him was a St. Patrick's Day party I threw, inviting some Irish friends. I made corned beef and cabbage to go with tales of Paddy's Day in Galway. My meal was a hit and has found a special place in each of our hearts—for me, carrying on a memory of a yearly holiday with my family, and for Mike, my husband, an understanding of the place I come from. Now we make it for all special occasions with a Celtic flair. Its rustic, bold flavours seem to really appeal to our guests. It's a very simple recipe, but the secret is in the time you take to cook it. The meat becomes very tender with long cooking and the broth is used to cook the cabbage. Enjoy!

1–2 Tbsp vegetable oil
one 3–5-lb piece corned beef brisket, rinsed and dried
4–5 cans beer (ale works best)
1 head savoy cabbage, coarsely sliced

› SERVES 6–8

IN a Dutch oven or large heavy saucepan, heat oil over medium-high heat. Brown brisket on both sides to seal in the flavour. Pour in enough beer to cover meat. Bring to a boil, lower heat and simmer, covered, for 5 hours. When done, the meat should be fork-tender.

REMOVE meat from broth, cover and keep warm. Bring broth to a boil. Stir in cabbage and gently simmer for no more than 5 minutes. Drain cabbage and slice meat. Serve sliced meat and cabbage with mustard and lots of mashed potatoes!

> BLACK PEPPER BEEF TENDERLOIN STIR-FRY
WITH KING OYSTER MUSHROOMS

ALLEN LIU, *Kirin Seafood Restaurants*

I started working in restaurant kitchens in Hong Kong when I was thirteen. I loved wonderful gourmet cooking, but my family was poor, so by learning how to cook in professional restaurants, I was able to follow my passion. I did three years of apprenticeship, including cleaning the kitchen, washing the dishes, etc., before I was allowed to begin cooking. By 1989, I was a well-known chef in Hong Kong, and Kirin recruited me for their restaurant in downtown Vancouver. Now I'm the chief chef of four Kirin Seafood Restaurants, overseeing eighty chefs. This recipe is the first dish that my mentor taught me to make in Hong Kong. When I prepare it now, it brings back fond memories of the man who taught me to be not only a master chef, but also a good leader and kind person who cares about all of my staff.

> SERVES 4

SAUCE: Mix all sauce ingredients, stirring until smooth. Set aside.

STIR-FRY: Pour 1 teaspoon of the oil into a preheated frying pan over medium heat. Fry sliced garlic until golden brown. Remove and set aside.

ADD another 1 teaspoon of the oil and heat to medium heat. Stir-fry the beef until half cooked (about 40 seconds). Remove and set aside.

ADD and heat the final 1 teaspoon oil. Add mushrooms, green onion, pepper, minced garlic and the deep-fried sliced garlic. Stir-fry for about 40 seconds. Add beef and the sauce and stir-fry until sauce is totally reduced. Remove and place on chopped lettuce on a serving plate.

SAUCE
1 tsp light soy sauce
½ tsp granulated sugar
½ tsp cornstarch
2 Tbsp chicken broth

STIR-FRY
1 Tbsp cooking oil, divided
4 cloves garlic, thinly sliced
10 oz beef tenderloin, cut into ¾-inch cubes
4 oz king oyster mushrooms, cut to about ¼ × 1 × 1½ inches
2 oz green onion, cut into 2-inch lengths
¼ tsp black pepper, crushed
1 clove garlic, minced

GARNISH
4 oz lettuce, chopped into 1-inch squares

GUYANESE PEPPER POT

CHARLENE WHARTON

This is one of my favourite family recipes from Guyana. My dad learned how to make pepper pot from his grandmother, though traditionally the recipe would have been handed down from mother to daughter. Many people make it at Christmastime, but it's not really a Christmas dish. Nowadays, my dad, Ecliffe, makes it for special occasions like Christmas, Thanksgiving, birthdays—any great family get-together. It's always a treat when I visit my parents and pepper pot is served!

› SERVES 6

WASH meat and scrape ends of bones (to ensure that no bone flakes end up in Pepper Pot). Cut off visible fat. Heat oil in a large sauté pan that has a lid. Brown meat on all sides. Add onion, garlic, tomatoes, cinnamon, cloves, parsley, oregano, a sprinkling of salt and a few grinds of pepper. If you prefer spicy, you can add hot chilies with the rest of the spices. Lower the heat, cover and let simmer until meat is fork tender. This will take about 1½ to 2 hours. Add casareep and sugar and stir well. Remove peppers and cinnamon stick before serving. Allow to cool and skim off fat. For best flavour, allow to sit in the refrigerator for 24 hours. Can be served with rice or bread. (I love a thick slice of bread to soak up the sauce!)

2 lb beef short ribs or oxtail, cut into 2-inch pieces
1 Tbsp vegetable oil
1 large onion, diced
8–10 cloves garlic, crushed
2 medium tomatoes, cored and diced
1 cinnamon stick
6–8 whole cloves
2 Tbsp chopped parsley
1½ tsp dried oregano or 1 Tbsp fresh oregano, chopped
salt and pepper, to taste
hot chilies, to taste (optional)
casareep, about 3 Tbsp (see note)
2 tsp granulated sugar

NOTE Casareep is a thick syrup prepared by boiling down juice from cassava tubers with sugar, cloves and cinnamon. It comes from Guyana and is available in specialty stores like Caribbean Market at 1003 Royal Avenue, New Westminster.

> BOBOTIE
(SPICED MEAT AND FRUIT CASSEROLE)

SHARON HABIB

The beloved traditional dish of any South African you speak to—including me—is bound to be bobotie (you pronounce it "bubootie"). While we proudly claim it as our own, its origins are actually Malaysian. In years gone by, when slavery was common practice, slaves were imported to South Africa from Malaysia. Once freed, they stayed, and taught the locals a thing or two about cooking with all the wonderful spices that found their way ashore from ships travelling the spice route around the tip of Africa to India. South Africa being a fruit-growing country, fruit finds its way into many meat, chicken and fish dishes, and bobotie is no exception. My mouth waters as I write. You simply must try it. The original recipe came from *The Complete South African Cookbook* by Magdaleen Van Wyk (pronounced "funvake"), but this version is updated with my own touches and extra spices, gleaned from the countless times I've made this dish.

> SERVES 8

PREHEAT the oven to 350°F. Soak the bread in ½ cup of the milk, squeeze to remove excess milk and mix the bread with the ground meat. Mix in all the other ingredients except butter or oil, eggs, remaining milk and bay leaves.

HEAT butter or oil in a frying pan and brown the meat mixture lightly. Turn out into a casserole dish. (You can freeze it at this point if you want.) Beat eggs and the remaining milk together and pour over the meat mixture. Garnish with bay leaves. Bake until set, about 45 to 50 minutes.

BOBOTIE is traditionally served with rice and these condiments: fruit chutney, sliced banana and dried coconut.

1 slice white bread
1 cup milk, divided
2 lb ground beef or lamb
1 medium onion, finely chopped
¾ cup seedless raisins
¾ cup blanched almonds, chopped
2 Tbsp whole apricot jam (I use more—it's that tendency to cook fruit with meat)
3 Tbsp fruit chutney
5 tsp lemon juice
2 tsp curry powder
1 tsp turmeric
2 tsp salt
1 cinnamon stick
10 whole cloves
2 tsp butter or vegetable oil
3 large eggs
2 bay leaves

HAPPINESS

(BRAISED PORK BELLY WITH BAMBOO SHOOTS)

CHOI KWAN NG

Bamboo shoots in Chinese sounds like "ha," and "ha" sounds like laughter. Whenever I eat this traditional Hakka dish, I think of my mother. (Hakka people are migratory tribes of ethnic Han people originating from central China.) It's the dish I remember her making for every Chinese New Year when I was little. After I was married (and not a very good cook yet) every time I visited my mother, she would make this dish for me and my family to enjoy, and to wish happiness among my family. Now I can prepare a dinner for ten without a lot of difficulty, and Happiness has become one of my family's favourite dishes. I make it for many occasions, not only for Chinese New Year. It has been almost nine years since I first tried to make this dish, and now my husband and daughters think it tastes as good as my mother's, but to me it still tastes different from my mom's. Maybe it's not the taste that is different, but the fact that I can no longer share this dish with my late mom.

10 oz bamboo shoots
   (one 300-g can)
5 Tbsp vegetable oil, divided
1½ lb pork belly, cut into
   pieces
2 slices fresh ginger
1 Tbsp Chinese cooking wine
1½ cups water
½ tsp salt
1½ tsp dark soy sauce
4½ tsp light soy sauce
1½ tsp granulated sugar

> SERVES 6

BRING a large pot of water to a boil. Drop in bamboo shoots, bring back to a boil for 2 minutes, remove and drain. When cool, cut into wedges and set aside.

HEAT a wok or large frying pan over high heat and add 3 tablespoons of the oil—oil should cover the bottom of the pan, so add more if necessary. Fry pork on both sides until slightly golden. Transfer to a tray lined with paper towels to absorb excess oil and set aside. Wipe out the pan and heat the remaining 2 tablespoons of oil. Sauté ginger over medium heat for 2 to 3 minutes, then add the fried pork belly and cook a few minutes. Deglaze the pan with the cooking wine, stirring up any browned bits on bottom of pan. Add water, salt, dark and light soy sauce and sugar. Stir well. Bring to a boil over high heat and add bamboo shoots. Reduce heat to medium-low. Cover and simmer for 1½ hours or until pork is tender.

> BBQ PORK

WITH GREEN BEANS IN BLACK BEAN SAUCE

ROSS MARTIN

This recipe speaks for itself, with origins in China and adaptation from a dish at one of Vancouver's most memorable Chinatown restaurants. But it is definitely a family recipe now. Many years ago, our favourite Chinese restaurant was the On On Tea Garden on Keefer Street. We found it years before Trudeau made it famous! We were sorry when it closed. One of our favourite dishes was their BBQ Pork with Green Beans in Black Bean Sauce. About ten years ago, I bought a Chinese cookbook and found a recipe for Stuffed Green Peppers with Black Bean Sauce. Reading through, I thought that if I started in the middle and made some changes it might be close … and it's almost perfect.

> SERVES 6

SAUCE: Mix all sauce ingredients well and set aside.

STIR-FRY: Blanch green beans briefly in boiling water. Drain and cut into 2-inch pieces. Set aside. Heat the sesame and vegetable oils in a wok or large sauté pan over medium-high heat. Brown the sliced BBQ pork, then remove and set aside. Reheat oil (add more sesame oil if needed for stir-frying), and add black beans, garlic, green onions and ginger. Stir-fry until fragrant and then add the sauce, the meat, and then the green beans. Simmer and cook, uncovered, until beans are tender. Serve over steamed rice.

SAUCE

1½ cups chicken broth
2 Tbsp soy sauce
2 Tbsp dry sherry
2 Tbsp sake
2 tsp cornstarch
¾ tsp granulated sugar
½ tsp salt
1 Tbsp Chinese black vinegar (the secret flavour!)

STIR-FRY

3 cups green beans, ends and strings removed
1 Tbsp sesame oil
1 Tbsp vegetable oil
¾–1 lb good Chinese BBQ pork, cut lengthwise and then cut into thin slices (about the size of a quarter), bones and excess fat removed
2 generous Tbsp Chinese fermented black beans, rinsed, drained and minced
2 generous Tbsp minced garlic
2 generous Tbsp minced green onions
1 Tbsp minced fresh ginger

B.C. CHOUCROUTE

MARIE FRANCO

My family came to Vancouver in 1966 from Germany. My mom's from Holland, my father is Spanish and I was born in Britain. My husband is unusual—born and bred in good old Burnaby, B.C.—but his grandparents came from the Ukraine and Britain. How's that for a typical Canadian mélange? This recipe for choucroute stems from my childhood in Germany (sauerkraut), my parents' Dutch and Spanish roots (sausages) and our hobby of seeking out the very best local ingredients for the meat, vegetables and wines. You can make it ahead of time; it's easy, hearty food that can be dressed up or down to suit the occasion and what's in your fridge, and it's a dish that is meant to bring family and friends to the table to share the bounty. Best of all, this recipe can be made well ahead of time; it's one pot, and makes a huge amount—enough to feed six or eight and still have leftovers for a couple of meals. Like so many one-pot meals, it gets more mellow and yummy after a few days. It's easy, yet unusual enough that even our foodie and wine-weenie friends think of it as a treat. How do you say bon appétit in Ukrainian?

> SERVES 6–8

OVER medium heat, melt butter in a large pot with a lid. Cook onions and garlic, stirring occasionally, until onions are translucent (about 10 minutes). Add wine and stock and bring to a boil. Reduce heat to simmer and add sauerkraut, bouquet garni, caraway seeds and juniper berries. Cover and simmer for 15 minutes. Add bacon and simmer for 15 minutes. Nestle sausage into sauerkraut, cover and simmer 30 minutes. Remove bouquet garni. Serve with one or more varieties of mustard as a wonderful condiment complement.

THIS DISH begs for a wine from its area of origin. A Riesling or Gewürztraminer from Germany or from the Alsace region of France would be perfect, as would one of the many solid efforts made with these grapes from B.C., Australia or Washington State.

2 Tbsp butter (or use duck fat, if you have it)

2 medium onions, chopped

2 cloves garlic, chopped

½ bottle dry white wine, such as Chardonnay

1 cup chicken stock

2½ lb sauerkraut, rinsed and drained

1 bouquet garni: 2 sprigs parsley and 1 bay leaf, tied together

½ tsp caraway seeds

8 juniper berries

½ lb thick smoked bacon, chopped into 1-inch pieces

1½ lb garlic sausage (whole or chopped, your preference)

NOTE Use any mix of smoked pork chops, bacon or sausages that suits you.

❯ RIBBE

(NORWEGIAN ROAST PORK)

RANDI GURHOLT-SEARY

For my father, Christmas was a time to connect with the childhood and family that he left behind in Norway in the 1950s. He would spend days preparing all of the baked goods prior to *Jule Aften* (Christmas Eve) and then make the main meal on the day. I loved to watch my engineer father, who was normally away at the office, with his white apron wrapped around him in our kitchen. It was from him that I learned how to prepare the traditional Jule Aften main course—Ribbe, the savoury pork dish! With him I learned just how to rub the beautiful large slab of pork side, with ribs, fat and skin intact, with a generous amount of salt and pepper; to score the skin and fat in a diamond pattern and press whole cloves into each cut; to roast it for the most part of the day and then broil the top until it rises and crisps just right. The smells of this dish told us all that it was Jule Aften. My son has taken part in preparing this traditional dish every year with me, in keeping with tradition. At my side he has learned about my childhood memories as well as his grandfather's. It has remained our touchstone to the past, present and future, with our heritage from Norway and family abroad. It is difficult to provide the cooking instructions on paper as I learned it by sight, sound and smell—and, more importantly, with the old Norwegian Christmas songs of my father inspiring and guiding me. However, here is my attempt.

pork loin roast
salt and pepper, to taste
whole cloves
water (¾ cup)

NOTE This recipe requires an advance special order with your butcher. Order a pork loin roast on the bone, of a size that suits your family—at least 5 pounds. Ask that they keep the ribs, fat and skin intact, and that they remove the chine bone and crack between the ribs for ease in carving.

❯ SERVES AS MANY AS THE SIZE OF ROAST YOU BUY

THE DAY before, wash the roast and pat dry. Cut and score the skin with a diamond pattern. Generously sprinkle with salt and pepper. Rub salt and pepper into the cut and scored fat and the underside of the ribs. Be generous. Just when you think you have done enough, add some more! Wrap and return to the refrigerator for cooking the next day.

ON Christmas Eve morning (or the day you wish to serve), preheat the oven to 400°F. Remove roast from the refrigerator. Sing to it your favourite song, remark on how beautiful it is and play holiday music in the background to celebrate the cooking of the pork. Place it on a rack in a roasting pan that will catch the drippings. If you think it needs a little more salt and pepper, feel free to add them. Place a pile of whole cloves on the counter. One by one, press them into the grooves of each diamond cut on the skin and fat, making a beautiful pattern. Add water to the bottom of the roasting pan. Wrap foil over the top of the pork and place the pan in the hot oven. Cook for about 1 hour and then reduce heat to 325°F. You will hear the fat start to crackle. Remember to check the meat every so often to see if it is happily roasting as expected. You can use the fat at the bottom of the pan to baste the pork occasionally and create a crisper skin.

AFTER about 3 to 4 hours of roasting, remove the foil. You must delight in the aromas and let the pork know how appreciative you are! It should be ready for crisping after about 5 to 7 hours of cooking, depending on its size. Baste again. To create the crispiest skin, place under the broiler for 5 to 10 minutes just before serving. Watch closely to make sure it doesn't burn! Serve whole on a large platter and cut into squares.

SERVE with *tutte baere* (lingonberries in Sweden or cranberries in Canada) and a glass of aquavit that has been chilled and kept in the freezer for the year in anticipation. Enjoy! This dish is delicious served cold on Christmas Day for breakfast! *God Jul* (Merry Christmas) *fra oss til dere* (from us to you)!

NOTE This is a special recipe in which the pork is cooked for a long time. Pork is at its best when thoroughly cooked, but it is not necessary to exceed an internal temperature of 160°F. Removing the meat from the oven when its internal temperature is 145°F to 150°F and allowing it to rest will bring the temperature up to 160°F, as it continues to cook in its own heat.

SINGAPORE STEAMBOAT

JANE McCALL

In 1979, my partner, Stuart, and I took a six-month backpacking trip around Southeast Asia. Among our many great memories of that trip is the fantastic street food we ate. Without a doubt, the street-food capital was Singapore. On numerous occasions we ate Singapore Steamboat, and the best place to eat it was Bugis Street—we sat at a table that was equipped with a gas-fired burner. A metal container that looked kind of like an angel-food-cake pan was placed over the burner and filled with chicken stock. Many small dishes of raw meats, dumplings and vegetables were brought to the table. Over the course of the evening, as we gawked at the transgendered ladies of the night who gyrated around us, we dipped, cooked and ate. It was wonderful. When we came home, we adapted the recipe for an electric fondue pot. Our kids love cooking their own dinner, and Singapore Steamboat has become our official celebration meal. One fondue pot works well for a maximum of four people, so if you do this for a party make sure you beg or borrow some extras.

> SERVES 4

NOTE If you are using a full-flavoured chicken stock, diluting it half and half with water is usually a good idea. The stock will reduce while the meal progresses, so you could end up with a stronger tasting and possibly overly salty stock. Also, the dipping foods will taste their best if they are not overpowered by the stock.

SOY-GINGER DIPPING SAUCE: Mix together all sauce ingredients and set aside.

FONDUE: Thoroughly heat chicken stock, sliced ginger and green onion in a saucepan and then place in an electric fondue pot, keeping the stock very hot throughout the meal. Arrange wontons, meat,

SOY-GINGER DIPPING SAUCE
½ cup soy sauce
1-inch piece ginger, finely grated
1 Tbsp granulated sugar
1–2 Tbsp finely chopped fresh cilantro

FONDUE
4 cups diluted chicken stock (see note), homemade is best
¾-inch piece of ginger, sliced
2–3 green onions, sliced
12–18 wontons or other dumplings that are suitable for boiling
10–14 oz sirloin steak, thinly sliced
8–12 raw prawns
1 bunch baby bok choy, separated into serving-sized pieces
8 oz green beans, topped and tailed
12 mushrooms, cleaned and left whole
steamed rice for 4
Chinese chili-garlic sauce for dipping (store-bought)
soy-ginger dipping sauce (recipe provided)
1 egg

prawns and vegetables on serving plates. Pour both dipping sauces into individual saucers or small bowls for each diner. Provide a bowl of steamed rice for each person. Make sure each person has at least one fondue fork and a small dipping basket (available in Asian food stores) for retrieving wontons and other items from the stock. Cook the food and eat with the dipping sauces and the rice. When all the food is gone, break the egg into the stock and swirl it. Serve the egg soup to finish the meal.

➤ DESSERTS

SCHOGGI MAKARÖNLI
(CHOCOLATE MACAROONS)

JUDY BOXLER

In 1975, while we were living in Switzerland, our friend Ursula Kieliger served my husband and me the most delicious assortment of Christmas cookies. Among them were my favourite: Schoggi Makarönli (chocolate macaroons). Ursula remembered making Christmas cookies with her mother when she was a child and showed me how her mother had used two spoons to form the round balls for the macaroons. This recipe always brings back memories of the warmth of Ursula's kitchen, which emanates as much from her enthusiasm for enjoying the good things in life as from her stove. Schoggi Makarönli have become one of my standard Christmas cookies. I also keep a stash in the freezer for unexpected guests or a simple dessert at any time of the year. They are always a hit!

7 oz good quality chocolate (e.g., Lindt 85%)
1 lb hazelnuts or almonds, ground
1 cup minus 1 Tbsp granulated sugar
5 egg whites *or* 3 whole large eggs

> MAKES 80 SMALL COOKIES

PREHEAT the oven to 325°F. Line baking sheets with parchment paper.

IN the top of a double boiler, over simmering water, melt the chocolate. Add ground nuts and sugar and combine. Blend in egg whites, or whole eggs if using that option.

DROP the batter onto the parchment paper by the teaspoonful and shape into balls. Bake for 15 minutes. Carefully remove from baking sheet, as the cookies crumble easily. These cookies freeze well.

> BOOZELS

CAROL CURRY

My maternal grandmother, Anna Scheirich, was a legendary cook. I believe her recipes all originated from her childhood home in Mariolana, Yugoslavia, where German was her native tongue. She and my grandfather, Peter, immigrated to Canada and settled in a predominantly German community in Winnipeg. Eventually she learned English well enough, but her mispronunciations were often amusing. For example, we were astonished to be told we had relatives in "Red China," but she had really been trying to say Regina. Mispronunciations aside, Anna was known for her honesty, financial shrewdness and, most famously, her cooking. A family favourite of hers were cookies she called Boozels. As I grew older and more interested in the art of cooking, I asked her for the Boozel recipe. She said, "Tell me when you'll come and we'll make them." When I arrived for the cooking lesson, she began deftly scooping flour onto her pastry cloth with her hand. As she reached for the next ingredient, I was astonished to realize that the recipe was not written down anywhere. I stopped her long enough to say, "Granny, can we measure that flour and anything else you put in the cookies so I'll remember?" Thus, the recipe for Boozels was born. My daughters now make Boozels for their families. I am honoured to share this recipe with you in memory of my grandmother.

COOKIES
1 cup granulated sugar
1 cup butter, softened
2 large eggs, well beaten
2½ cups all-purpose flour
½ tsp salt
½ tsp baking soda
1 tsp cream of tartar
¼ tsp nutmeg

GARNISH
¼ cup finely ground nuts (preferably hazelnuts or almonds)
1 Tbsp granulated sugar
1 egg white, beaten

> MAKES SEVENTY 2-INCH COOKIES

COOKIES: Preheat the oven to 400°F. Dust baking sheets lightly with flour. Beat butter with the 1 cup sugar until light and fluffy. Add beaten eggs. Set aside. Sift dry ingredients together. Gradually add dry ingredients to wet ingredients until blended. Do not over-mix! Chill dough for 1 hour.

ROLL dough out to ¼-inch thickness. Using fancy cookie cutters, cut dough into shapes and place on the floured baking sheet, leaving at least 1 inch of space between them. Mix together ground nuts and the 1 Tbsp granulated sugar. Brush a spot of beaten egg white in the middle of or along each cookie. Sprinkle with the nut mixture. Bake for about 10 minutes, or until lightly browned at edges. Cool and enjoy!

AUNT RAGNILD'S OVERNIGHT COOKIES

CLARA HILL

In 1928, when I was a child in rural Saskatchewan, my Aunt Ragnild, Uncle Einar and their three children came from Norway and lived with us on the farm until they found their own home. There were eight children in our family so we became quite a crowd to cook meals for every day! I remember my aunt preparing these cookies at night and putting the dough in a cool place to be baked the next day when the oven was hot. After their family left us, the cookie recipe remained and was ever known as Aunt Ragnild's Overnight Cookies.

½ cup butter, softened
¾ cup brown sugar
1 large egg
½ tsp baking soda
2 cups all-purpose flour
½ cup chopped walnuts, toasted

> MAKES 24 COOKIES

CREAM butter and sugar together well. Add egg and mix thoroughly. Add baking soda, flour and nuts and mix well. Form into a log shape about 2 inches in diameter. Wrap in wax paper and refrigerate overnight.

THE NEXT DAY, preheat the oven to 350°F. Line baking sheets with parchment paper. Slice the dough log into about ¼-inch-thick cookies. Bake about 10 minutes, or until pale golden brown. Cool on a rack.

FENWICK FLORENTINE COOKIES

PENNY HANNAH

My mother taught me how to make these wonderful fruit cookies. Months prior to Christmas, our kitchen would be filled with the aromas of Christmas cake and Fenwick Florentine Cookies. My mother remembers her grandmother from England teaching her how to make them. I make them every year, and now my grown children make them, too. The taste of fruit with chocolate is delicious, and one of my best friends always asks me for a package at Christmas. We also love these at tea time.

> MAKES 36 COOKIES

PREHEAT the oven to 350°F. Line a baking sheet with parchment paper.

PUT fruit and flour into a food processor fitted with a steel blade. Pulse on/off to chop the fruit into pieces about ¼ inch in size. Add sugar, nuts, honey, salt, vanilla and melted butter and pulse again until the fruit and nut pieces are about ⅛ inch. By now the mixture will be forming a ball. Remove and form dough into 1-inch balls. Place on baking sheet, about 2 inches apart. Flatten each cookie with a fork dipped into cold water. Bake about 8 minutes, until set. Cool on a rack.

ONCE the cookies have cooled, melt chocolate over hot, not boiling, water and stir until smooth. Spread a layer of chocolate on the bottom of each cookie and place chocolate side up on a baking sheet until chocolate is set.

NOTE Sometimes I reduce the flour to ⅓ cup and add ⅓ cup of Rice Krispies cereal after the dough has been blended. Sometimes I will also presoak the fruit in 2 tablespoons of brandy.

1¼ cups packed mixed dried fruit of best quality:
   ¾ cup pitted dates, roughly chopped
   ¼ cup raisins
   ¼ cup apricots, roughly chopped
½ cup flour
4 Tbsp brown sugar
½ cup pecans or almonds
4 Tbsp honey (best quality)
⅛ tsp salt
½ tsp vanilla extract
3 Tbsp unsalted butter, melted
6–8 oz semisweet chocolate (about 1 cup chocolate pieces)

HOKEY POKIES

ALISON HALE

My grandmother was a war bride. She brought many recipes with her from England but my favourite is the one that used to make us laugh and dance in the kitchen. These cookies had the best name a kid could ask for: they were truly called Hokey Pokies! I have a little girl and she has just learned how to do the Hokey Pokey, so I thought that it was time to introduce her to the "other" Hokey Pokies. Now, as soon as she sees the cookies, she does her "turn around" and then devours them. When I asked Grama for the recipe last night this is what I got:

½ cup butter
¾ cup granulated sugar
1 cup flour
pinch of cream of tartar
1 Tbsp warm milk
1 Tbsp Rogers Golden Syrup
  (cane sugar syrup)
pinch of baking soda

> MAKES 36 COOKIES

So here is a cookie recipe
That tells you at a glance
That after you have baked them
You will do a little dance

They are called the "Hokey Pokies"
And they come from Grama's kitchen
They will up and make you tap your feet
And get you cooking in the kitchen

You take a ½ cup of butter and ¾ cup of sugar
And mix it all about
Take 1 cup of flour and a pinch of cream of tartar
And add it all together
You do the Hokey Pokey, and you turn yourself around!

You take a tablespoon of warm milk and 1 tablespoon of syrup
And swirl it all about
You take a pinch of soda and add it to the milk and syrup
And you wait until they fluff
You do the Hokey Pokey, and you turn yourself around!

You take the entire ingredients and mix them all about
Roll into balls and take a fork and flatten them out
And you cook for 35 to 45 minutes and in the meantime
You do the Hokey Pokey, and you turn yourself around!

Bake slowly at 250°F because that's what it is all about!
You do the Hokey Pokey, and you turn yourself around!

MATILDA ROEDDE'S GINGERBREAD COOKIES

KATHERINE LAWRENCE

One of my favourite family recipes comes from my great-grandmother, Matilda Roedde, who immigrated to Canada from the island of Heligoland in the North Sea, off Germany. When I was a child, we gathered every Christmas to make and decorate my great-grandmother's fantastic gingerbread. We kids would help prepare the ingredients and take turns mixing them. Accurate measurement of the ingredients was an absolute requirement, and when it came to mixing, the number of turns per child was strictly and rigorously apportioned. Making a good-luck wish was part of the ritual, formally blessed by the household gods with the rich, gingery aromas from the oven. Our gingerbread men, quite apart from the delight of eating them, were also essential decoration for our Christmas tree. The family secret that I want to share with you is the magical ingredient required to make the sweet gingerbread extra crispy. Great-Grandmother added a quarter of a cup of bacon fat, decanted straight from the frying pan, to the butter. Today that might be considered a no-no, but it's a challenge you might like to take on this Christmas, for the best gingerbread that you have ever tasted.

P.S. My great-grandmother's house, the Roedde House, is a museum in Vancouver's West End. To experience an old-fashioned Vancouver Christmas, visit the house during the festive season for traditional carol singing and other wonderful seasonal family events.

½ cup granulated sugar
¼ cup bacon fat
½ cup butter *or* ¾ cup butter
   if bacon fat is eliminated
1 large egg
¼ cup dark molasses
2¼ cups all-purpose flour
1 tsp baking soda
1 tsp cinnamon
1 Tbsp ground ginger
raisins for decorating

> MAKES THIRTY 4-INCH GINGERBREAD MEN,
OR MANY MORE SMALLER COOKIES

IN a mixing bowl, cream together sugar, bacon fat and butter very well. Add egg and molasses, stirring to combine thoroughly. In a separate bowl, stir together flour, baking soda, cinnamon and ginger, then mix into the creamed ingredients. Form the dough into a ball, flatten, wrap in plastic and chill for at least 1 hour.

PREHEAT the oven to 350°F. Line baking sheets with parchment paper. On a floured surface, roll out the dough to a little thinner than ¼ inch (for the crispiest cookies) and cut with cookie cutters. Re-roll the scraps and cut more cookies. Decorate with raisins. Bake for 10 minutes. Cool on a rack.

› EDYTHE'S PAVLOVA

ANDREA MULLIN

On my first visit to New Zealand, my Kiwi mother-in-law taught me how to make a "proper" Pavlova. The ingredients are few and simple, but there's a definite knack to the method. Edythe owned a coffee lounge in Auckland for a number of years and baked two pavs a day for longer than she'd like to remember, but she still whips one up for every family event. Hers are the best, and as I learned from a pro, mine are pretty good too. Pav became my trademark dessert whenever we went to a potluck, but that changed when we moved to New Zealand for eight years. I felt a bit odd—as if taking coals to Newcastle—so I didn't make too many while living there. Now that we're back in Vancouver, however, my pav-baking days are here again!

6 large egg whites, room temperature
6 Tbsp cold water
2 cups granulated sugar
2 tsp white vinegar
2 tsp vanilla extract
6 tsp cornstarch
whipped cream for garnish
sliced fresh fruit for decoration

› SERVES 12

GREASE a large rimless baking sheet with vegetable shortening. Cover with parchment or baking paper. Grease the paper and cover with a second layer of paper. Preheat the oven to 300°F.

BEAT egg whites until stiff. Add cold water and beat again. Add sugar very, very *slowly* while still beating at high speed—this should take about 5 minutes. Scrape down the sides of the bowl. Using a slower beater speed, add vinegar, vanilla and cornstarch.

SCOOP the mixture into the centre of the prepared pan. The mixture should be piled high, with a diameter of only 6 to 8 inches, as it spreads while it bakes. Spend time shaping the sides, eliminating any bubbles that may form. Bake for 45 minutes. Turn the heat off, but leave the Pavlova in the oven to cool completely. This may take 4 to 5 hours.

JUST before serving, garnish the top with whipped cream and decorate with sliced kiwi, strawberries or any combination of colourful fruit.

NOTE A perfect pav should be crisp on the outside and soft and marshmallowy on the inside—not dry like a meringue.

GERMAN BLUEBERRY TORTE

LORI HAREID

When I was a child in Germany, my grandmother taught me to make this torte. She usually used blueberries, but out of season she made it with apples and it was equally delicious. Many years later, living here in Vancouver, I re-created the recipe from memory and it always seemed to work. I think of my grandmother with such fondness as my friends enjoy her dessert. Fresh blueberries are best.

> SERVES 8

PASTRY: Mix all ingredients in a food processor until the dough begins to hold together. Remove to a lightly floured surface and gather into a ball. Flatten a little and dust with flour. Wrap and chill for about 1 hour.

PREHEAT the oven to 425°F. Have a 9-inch springform pan on hand. Roll chilled dough into a thin circle and fit into the bottom and partway up the sides of the pan (about 1¼ inches to 1½ inches). It's a forgiving pastry, so if there is a small tear, press the edges together with your fingers. Chill while making filling.

FILLING: In a medium-sized bowl, mix sugar, flour and egg yolks thoroughly. In a separate bowl, whip the egg whites to stiff peaks, then fold into yolk mixture.

POUR blueberries into the base, making sure they stay within the pastry sides. Spread the egg mixture over berries. Bake 10 minutes, then reduce heat to 350°F and bake a further 35 minutes.

NOTE If using apples, 4 small to medium Golden Delicious work well. Slice peeled, cored apples very thinly and layer onto the pastry bottom. Spread topping over top and bake the same as for berries.

PASTRY
5 Tbsp unsalted butter, room temperature
⅓ cup granulated sugar
1 large egg
1¼ cups all-purpose flour
1¼ tsp baking powder
1 tsp vanilla extract

FILLING
2 Tbsp granulated sugar
2 Tbsp all-purpose flour
3 large eggs, separated
fresh blueberries or sliced apples, about 3 cups (see note)

VEL'S RHUBARB CRISP

SHERYL MacKAY, CBC Radio's *North by Northwest*

My father had a prize rhubarb patch all the years I was growing up in Prince Edward Island. Now, I don't think rhubarb is usually a demanding plant, but he babied that patch, turning the soil around it carefully each spring and mulching it with all the shells from our lobster feeds and clam bakes. It was a lovely red rhubarb, and whether it was the tender care, the very smelly mulch or just the variety, it flourished and was delicious. My father loved rhubarb, and most of all he loved my mother's rhubarb crisp, and that was a love he passed on to us. Mom got this recipe from her mother. It's simple but delicious and to this day when I go home, any time of year, Mom will be sure to have a crisp cooling on the counter. My brother and I have been known to just eat it right out of the baking dish while it's still warm (only when no one is looking). I like it unadorned. It involves one of my favourite foods and something I love in most any form: oatmeal. Guess it's in the Scottish genes.

4 cups chopped rhubarb, cut into 1-inch pieces
2–3 Tbsp water, or more if rhubarb is dry
½ cup granulated sugar, or more to taste
⅓ cup butter, softened
½ cup all-purpose flour
½ cup rolled oats
¾ cup brown sugar

> SERVES 6–8

PREHEAT the oven to 350°F. Butter a deep 6-cup baking dish, or an 8-inch square pan. Mix rhubarb, water and granulated sugar in a bowl and pour into the buttered baking dish. In a separate bowl, cream butter. Mix in flour, oats and brown sugar to make a crumbly topping. Spread topping over rhubarb. Bake in the oven for about 35 to 40 minutes, or until the rhubarb is gently bubbling and the topping is lightly browned.

THIS dessert is not only delicious, but adaptable. You can use orange juice instead of the water with the rhubarb, and you can use apples instead of rhubarb, or a mixture of both fruits. If you use apples, it's nice to add 1 teaspoon cinnamon to the topping. You can also add ½ cup ground almonds to the topping, or ⅓ cup toasted wheat germ, for added flavour and nutrition.

PINK DESSERT

PAOLA QUIRÓS CRUZ

This pink dessert comes from my great-great-grandmother who enjoyed its tasty, soft texture every year on her birthday. Pachita, my great-great-grandmother, was always delighted when the girls in the kitchen made this dessert with love for her birthday. Since then my family has eaten it on other special occasions in her memory. This recipe reminds me of scenes from my childhood when I'm far away from my birthplace of Bogotá.

Cáqueza, a town near Bogotá with plenty of guava trees, was where my grandfather was born and my great-great-grandmother and my great-grandmother lived. They lived in a spacious and charming house with a marvellous garden in the centre. The most wonderful part of the house was the kitchen. A wood-fired oven and stove were the magical instruments used by the girls who helped in the kitchen—plus Rosalbina, my grandpa's mother—to make cakes, cookies, desserts, yogurt and other extraordinary dishes for special occasions. I learned to enjoy the pink dessert when the farmers brought a big box of guavas to the house. The sweet and aromatic smell of the ripe guavas and their tender pink meat awakened my senses. I was an observer in the kitchen. At my age, in that time, it was dangerous to be near the stove, even though my eyes were captivated with the way the ladies of the house started to prepare the pink dessert. Nowadays I make this dessert, which was passed on orally by my family for generations, to remember my childhood in that cozy house and the first steps that guided me to my passion for cooking.

> SERVES 6–8

NOTE Although fresh guavas are the first choice in making this dessert, the pink-fleshed ones are not readily available in Vancouver much of the year. You can substitute pure mango juice (not a mango drink). Your dessert will then be pale yellow, not pink!

¼ cup cornstarch
1 cup granulated sugar, divided
2 cups whole milk, cold
4 large eggs, separated
5–6 fresh guavas, peeled (see note)
2 envelopes (2 Tbsp total) unflavoured gelatin
¼ cup boiling water

PREHEAT the oven to 350°F.

IN a saucepan, mix cornstarch and ½ cup of the sugar well and gradually stir in the cold milk. Over medium heat, stir the mixture constantly with a wooden spoon until it thickens, about 7 to 10 minutes. Remove the pan from the heat. Beat egg yolks in a small bowl. Beating constantly, drizzle several tablespoons of the hot mixture into the yolks, and then add the egg-yolk mixture back into the hot mixture, again stirring constantly. Return the saucepan to low heat and continue beating for 2 to 3 minutes. Remove from the heat and pour the mixture into an ovenproof square glass dish.

WHILE the mixture is cooling, purée the peeled guavas in a blender and strain out the seeds. Measure out ½ cup of juice. Beat egg whites until frothy and gradually add the other ½ cup of sugar until they form stiff, glossy peaks.

POUR half of the guava juice into a small bowl and sprinkle gelatin over; do not stir. Allow gelatin to soften for 5 minutes. Pour in the boiling water and stir until gelatin is melted. Add remaining juice to gelatin and gently stir into egg whites. Finally, pour the guava-and-egg-white mixture onto the yolk mixture and bake 10 minutes. Cool on a rack and chill before serving. (Note: the two mixtures will combine in the cold.)

THAI APPLE PIE

LYNDA HENDRICKSON

Several years ago I was working on a research vessel as a baker. We were working in the Arctic and supplies of fresh fruit were starting to run low. I was baking apple pies (six to be exact) at the request of the chef and when I added the spices to the apples, I added five-spice powder instead of cinnamon by mistake. I had already added the nutmeg. Of course the apples, sugar and spices were mixed before I realized what I'd done. Because I couldn't toss the apple mixture, I decided to experiment. There was a new Thai café in Victoria at the time and I had fallen in love with the creative use of lime in recipes, so in went the lime. To make it a spectacular dessert, I made a Grand Marnier glaze for the cooked pies—and the rest is history. It soon became a requested favourite. I think our exposure to Asian flavours here on the West Coast saved my day.

PIE
8 cooking apples, peeled, cored and sliced
¾ cup granulated sugar
2 Tbsp all-purpose flour
1 tsp five-spice powder
pinch of ground nutmeg
zest of 4 limes, plus the juice of 2
pastry for a double-crust pie

1 egg yolk
1 Tbsp melted butter

GLAZE
½ cup icing sugar
1 Tbsp cream
1 Tbsp Grand Marnier

> SERVES 8

PIE: Preheat the oven to 450°F. Mix apples, sugar, flour, five-spice powder, nutmeg, zest and lime juice, and let sit for 10 minutes.

ROLL out 2 pie crusts. Place the first in a 9-inch glass pie plate. Fill with the apple mixture. Place the second crust on top and crimp the edges. With a sharp knife, cut six 1-inch slits around the centre of the top crust. Whisk egg yolk and melted butter together and brush onto the top. Put the pie in the oven for 10 minutes, then reduce heat to 350°F and bake for another 35 minutes. When done, the top should be golden and the apples tender when pierced with the tip of a sharp knife. Set on a rack to cool.

GLAZE: Mix all ingredients well and drizzle on the pie about ten minutes after it comes out of the oven.

➤ FIG PLATZ

LOIS KLASSEN

This is a traditional Mennonite recipe with a Vancouver twist. I invented it in response to the
mature and very prolific fig tree that grows in our backyard. I love
the tree because it predates our nineteen-year-old Kits duplex and
reminds me that there is a heritage of Mediterranean immigrants
here. Back to the recipe... *platz* is a familiar Mennonite dessert. It is
usually made with plums and apricots in season. I have found, however that figs are even better than the traditional fruit. They seem to
make the dessert softer, sweeter and lovely to look at. I have based
this recipe on my grandmother's version. She was born in Russia and
spent most of her life in Manitoba.

2½ cups all-purpose flour
2 tsp baking powder
1½ cups granulated sugar,
    divided
½ tsp salt
1 cup margarine or butter,
    cold and cubed
2 large eggs
1 tsp vanilla extract
¾ cup milk
2 tsp orange zest
ripe fresh figs (about 20),
    cut in half (top to bottom)

➤ SERVES 12 OR MORE

PREHEAT the oven to 350°F. Use a non-stick 10 × 15 inch jelly-roll pan.
If your pan does not have a non-stick surface, grease with shortening
and dust with flour.

IN a large bowl mix together flour, baking powder, 1 cup of the sugar,
and salt. Cut in margarine or butter until the pieces are the size of
small peas. Set 1 cup of the crumbed mixture aside for the topping. In
a small bowl, mix eggs, vanilla and milk. Stir the wet ingredients into
the crumb mixture. Stir in orange zest. Spread mixture in the pan.
Arrange figs with the open side up in rows. They should be close together but not touching, so that the cake can be cut into individual
pieces after baking. Make the topping by mixing the reserved crumb
mixture with the remaining ½ cup sugar. Sprinkle the topping evenly
over the fruit. Bake for 40 to 45 minutes, or until browned and a
toothpick comes out clean. Once cool, cut into dessert-sized squares,
each featuring a fig half. Of course, it can be served with ice cream.

VARIATION: (not authentically Mennonite) Before adding the topping,
drizzle a bit of brandy on the centre of each fig.

▸ VINATERTA

LEANNE DYCK

When I was growing up, Christmas was a joyous time of family gatherings, traditions, good cheer and food. Delicious smells poured forth from Mom's kitchen. This was her opportunity to showcase mouthwatering talent. Two desserts were at the centre of these festivities: English Pud to celebrate my dad's heritage, and my mom's recipe for Icelandic Vinaterta. Not surprisingly, Mom had been given the roots of her recipe from her mom, Grandma Olafson. Grandma's recipe loudly proclaimed its Icelandic heritage with its strong ethnic taste. Mom slightly toned down the recipe to make it more palatable for her husband. I, too, far preferred Mom's recipe. Years passed and I fell in love. Christmas was the test for my Mennonite boyfriend. How would he react to my large extended family? To Vinaterta? To my delight, he seemed at home in the company of my family. Next, he was served a piece of Vinaterta. The first bite was foreign to him. He turned the tastes around in his mouth. Would he finish his piece?

"It's okay if you don't finish it. It's a unique taste," my mom offered.

"Oh no, I like it." He finished it. "May I have another piece, please?"

Later that year we were married. Vinaterta was our wedding cake.

▸ SERVES 12–16

FILLING: Place prunes in a saucepan and add enough water to cover. Bring to a boil, lower heat, cover and simmer until prunes are very soft and most of the water has evaporated. Put through a food mill or purée in a blender. Add sugar and cardamom (if using), stir to combine and set aside to cool.

FILLING
2½ cups pitted prunes (1 lb/454 g)
1 cup sugar
1 tsp ground cardamom (optional)

LAYERS
½ cup unsalted butter, room temperature
1¼ cups sugar
2 large eggs
1 tsp vanilla
3–3½ cups all-purpose flour (or more if needed)
3 tsp baking powder
pinch of salt
½ cup milk

ALMOND ICING (OPTIONAL)
1 cup icing sugar
1 Tbsp butter, softened
1½ tsp milk
1¼ tsp almond extract

LAYERS: Preheat the oven to 375°F. Line cookie sheets with parchment paper. Cream butter and sugar in a large mixing bowl until fluffy. Add eggs one at a time, beating well after each addition. Stir in vanilla. Combine 3 cups of flour with the baking powder and salt, and add alternately with milk to the creamed mixture, beginning and ending with flour. If dough is sticky, add a little more flour to make rolling easier.

DIVIDE dough into 8 equal portions. On a floured surface, roll each portion into an 8-inch round about 1/4 inch in thickness. Place two rounds on a cookie sheet. Bake for 8 to 10 minutes or until slightly golden and done. Cool on a wire rack and repeat with the rest of the dough. Be sure to let the cookie sheet cool off completely before repeating with the next rounds.

ASSEMBLE by placing a round on a serving plate and spreading a layer of prunes over, using approximately 1/3 cup. Repeat, stacking rounds and layering with prunes, ending with your best-looking round on top. The layers will be crisp but will soften with the filling. If desired you can top with a thin layer of almond icing. Store in a tightly covered tin for a few days before cutting. It will also freeze well.

ALMOND ICING: Mix all icing ingredients together and spread on the top round.

AUNT POLLY'S CASSADETTI

DON GENOVA,
The Early Edition's "Pacific Palate" on CBC Radio

This Sicilian recipe is hard to find in cookbooks, where the pastries are usually called *cassateddi*. But my family always called them cassadetti, probably a variation owing to the many dialects of Italian found throughout Sicily. My recipe was brought to Canada from Italy by my grandmother, whom I never knew. But Aunt Polly kept the tradition going, and not too long before she passed away, she taught me how to make these ricotta-stuffed pastries. Now, when I have a special occasion, or just a craving for a childhood comfort food, I make them and keep the memory of my ancestors alive.

> **MAKES 24 PASTRIES**

DOUGH: In a large bowl, use your fingers to rub shortening into flour until the mixture is evenly blended. Make a well in the flour mixture and pour in salt, sugar and water. Make sure sugar dissolves before mixing further. Pull the flour mixture into the water mixture until you can form a ball. Knead lightly until smooth, then cover with plastic wrap and let rest for 15 minutes while you prepare the filling.

FILLING: Blend sugar and vanilla into ricotta cheese. The consistency should be smooth, not chunky.

TO ASSEMBLE: Separate the pasty into walnut-sized balls. Using all-purpose flour to prevent the dough from sticking to your surface, roll the balls into thin circles. Wet the rim of one edge of a pastry circle with a little water. Place a spoonful of filling onto the circle and fold the pastry over the filling to create a half-moon shape. Pinch the seam together to seal in a fluted shape. Repeat for the rest of the pastry.

DOUGH

¼ cup + 2 Tbsp vegetable shortening
4 cups cake flour
pinch of salt
½ cup granulated sugar
cold water (about 1 cup)
all-purpose flour for rolling out the rounds of dough

FILLING

½ cup granulated sugar
1 tsp vanilla extract
1 lb ricotta cheese
vegetable oil for frying
sugar for garnish

POUR ¼ inch vegetable oil into a frying pan and heat over medium-high heat. When oil is hot, fry the pastries in batches until golden-brown on both sides. Drain on paper towels and sprinkle with sugar while hot.

BEST eaten warm, almost straight from the pan!

SH'VESTKOVE' KNEDLIKY

(CZECH PLUM DUMPLINGS)

BĚLA HERMANEK

Imagine ripping open with your fork a steaming, fluffy pillow of a dumpling, topped with brown sugar, cottage cheese and melting butter. Then a juice the colour of bloody amber bursts out of it and the yellow flesh of a plum is exposed: the smell, the colours and the taste!

In the summer of 1968, while I was on student holidays in Switzerland, my country, Czechoslovakia, was invaded by the Warsaw Pact armies. Led by the Soviet Union, the Communist countries had to punish a member who strayed from the hard party line and got some liberal, truly "bohemian" ideas in its head—like the freedom of the press, for example. I was stranded in a foreign Western country. I lost my family, my friends, my language and my culture, not to mention the wonderful Czech cuisine. The Swiss had their cheese fondue and chocolate and many other good dishes, but their sober attitude was far from a bohemian one. I yearned for the well-known, predictable comfort of familiar meals. As an emigrant, I had so many adjustments to make and so much to learn, it took me a year to start cooking some typical, luscious Czech food. In the dorms and eatery of the University of Basel there were many groups of emigrants eyeing each other: there were the Greeks escaping a dictatorship, the Chileans secretly wishing for Communism, and us, emigrants from Czechoslovakia, escaping from Communism—a truly bizarre mixture! After mentioning my dumplings to a Czech student friend, he expressed a wish to be invited for such a familiar meal. Plum dumplings led to marriage! We immigrated to Canada ten years later. Every summer, when the plum season is in its peak, we freeze a lot of plums and then through the year invite a handful of special friends to a dumpling frenzy.

DUMPLINGS

1 cup cream cheese, room temperature
1 large egg
pinch of salt
2 cups all-purpose flour for the dough, plus more for working on the patties
water (about ⅔ cup)
20 small plums, washed and dried, or substitute apricots or strawberries

TOPPING

brown sugar
2% cottage cheese
½ cup butter, melted

DUMPLINGS: Put a large pot of salted water on to boil.

IN a large bowl, mix cream cheese with egg and salt until smooth. Add flour and water alternately until the dough begins to hold together. Then mix it with floured hands, until you get light, soft dough. Add additional flour only if the dough is sticky. (The more you work it and add flour, the harder the dough will get.)

USE a small spoon to cut out a chunk of the dough. Press it flat on a floured surface and wrap the soft round patty around a plum. The plum should be just coated with the dough and well sealed. Beginners always use too much dough. Practice makes perfect!

GENTLY lower the dumplings into the boiling water, without crowding, as each has to have room to swim up when done. Make sure they don't stick to the bottom of the pot during the first few minutes, or they will rip when unstuck. The result is still edible, but not so eye-pleasing. (If using frozen plums, let them swim on the surface for a minute longer to make sure the plums cook all the way through.) With a perforated spoon, scoop up the dumplings, nest them into a cozy bowl and cover to keep warm. Before serving, sprinkle with brown sugar, top with a heaping spoonful of cottage cheese and drizzle it all with melted butter.

I RECOMMEND you tuck a large paper napkin into your collar before cutting into a dumpling. And watch out for the stones! A pot of any kind of tea goes well with this dessert, as do wine and coffee. A plum brandy called slivovitz can crown this dish. If you really feel heroic, try to say it in Czech: *sh'vestkove' knedliky.* Enjoy!

CHRISTMAS PUDDING

JOAN KOEBEL

When my mother, Nora Allen, was a newlywed in 1937, she wrote to her father-in-law, Frederick, in England for his Christmas pudding recipe. She made it for many years with my dad, Eric, adding his own particular touch—the rum sauce. My mother, who was ninety-nine last year, is no longer able to cook Christmas dinner, but she has passed this special recipe on to me. The original recipe from my grandfather has its own special place on my kitchen wall. For me, this is a historical document. It connects me to a grandfather I never met—a grandfather whose beautiful script, descriptive language and willingness to share with his new daughter-in-law gives me a sense of extended family that I was not otherwise able to experience. A few years ago, my son Steve, wanting to contribute to our Christmas dinner, made Christmas pudding for dessert, using his great-grandfather's recipe. It was delicious! I wonder if my grandfather could have possibly anticipated this wonderful family treasure when he mailed this very special recipe to my mother in 1937.

> MAKES 3 PUDDINGS (EACH 5–6 CUPS)

NOTE Christmas puddings need to mature before serving, the optimum period being 6 to 8 weeks, so you will want to make them by the second or third week in November. Making them is a two-day process.

USING a very large mixing bowl, stir together flour, suet, spices, baking soda, salt and sugar. Gradually add the dried fruit, peel and nuts, then apples. In another bowl, beat together syrup, eggs, milk and whisky. Pour this liquid over the flour mixture and blend very well. Cover the bowl and leave overnight in the refrigerator.

2½ cups self-raising flour
1 lb beef suet, freshly shredded
1 tsp ground ginger
pinch of grated nutmeg
½ tsp baking soda
1 tsp salt
1 cup granulated sugar
3 cups seedless raisins
3 cups sultanas
3 cups currants
½ cup mixed candied peel
½ cup chopped almonds
2 fair-sized cooking apples, peeled, cored and finely chopped
2 Tbsp Rogers Golden Syrup (cane sugar syrup)
4 large eggs
1 tsp milk
½ cup Scotch whisky (or as Grandfather wrote—1 full wine glass!)

THE NEXT DAY, lightly grease three 5- to 6-cup heatproof pudding bowls. Pack the pudding mixture into the bowls. Cover the top of each pudding with a double layer of parchment paper and then a sheet of foil. Tie around with kitchen string. Place the bowls in a steamer set over boiling water and steam 6 hours. Check occasionally to see if more boiling water is needed. Allow to cool.

REMOVE all coverings and replace with fresh ones. Store in a cool place until Christmas. Freeze pudding(s) you will not be using at Christmas or giving away.

TO SERVE, steam 2 to 3 hours, depending on the size of the bowl. Carefully unmold, garnish and serve with cream, ice cream or the sauce of your choice.

BAKED COTTAGE PUDDING

ALICE SPURRELL

I am the eldest daughter in a family of seven children and my mom spent much of her day preparing meals for us. My father loved his meals, and he especially loved dessert. Traditional British desserts were our family favourites, because my grandfather was Welsh (he came to Nova Scotia with the English army when he was sixteen years old) and my grandmother was Scottish. Cookies were acceptable for evening tea, but dessert was always a warm offering. I remember many wonderful things—apple pie made with brown sugar, lemon meringue pie, golden cake with boiled icing and toasted coconut, baked lemon pudding, rice pudding and bread pudding. My very favourite was always Cottage Pudding in its many variations, baked in an old 12-inch frying pan. Serve it with warm Brown-Sugar Sauce, with fresh berries and whipped cream or as an upside-down cake.

> SERVES 8–10

PUDDING: Preheat the oven to 350°F. Grease a deep, 8-inch round cake pan.

IN a medium bowl, mix flour with baking powder and salt. Sift twice more and set aside.

IN a large bowl, cream butter and gradually add sugar, mixing until light and fluffy. Add egg gradually, mixing thoroughly. In a small bowl, add vanilla to milk. Alternate adding the flour mixture and the milk mixture to the batter, beginning and ending with the flour. Combine lightly after each addition. Pour the batter into the cake pan and spread evenly.

BAKE for about 50 minutes, or until the cake begins to pull away from the pan and springs back when you prod it gently with your finger.

PUDDING

1½ cups sifted
   all-purpose flour
2½ tsp baking powder
¼ tsp salt
5 Tbsp butter, softened
¾ cup granulated sugar
1 large egg, beaten
½ tsp vanilla extract
½ cup milk

BROWN-SUGAR SAUCE

1 Tbsp cornstarch
¼ cup brown sugar
pinch of salt
1 cup boiling water
1 Tbsp butter
½ tsp vanilla extract

BROWN-SUGAR SAUCE: Mix cornstarch, brown sugar and salt together in a small pot. Gradually stir in boiling water. Cook over low heat for about 8 minutes, stirring occasionally. At serving time, add butter a little at a time and vanilla. Stir until butter is melted. Serve over the warm Cottage Pudding.

UPSIDE-DOWN CAKE VARIATIONS: Many fruits may be used for this cake—sliced fresh apples, peaches, plums or pears; pitted cherries, or chopped rhubarb. Canned fruit, such as pears, peaches or pineapple, will work well too.

BUTTER the 8-inch cake pan, spread ¼ cup brown sugar over the bottom and dot with 2 Tbsp butter. Place in the oven for a few minutes until the butter melts. Arrange the prepared fruit over the sugar mixture, then spoon the cake batter over the fruit and spread carefully. Bake in the 350°F oven for 1 hour. Serve with whipped cream.

TRES LECHES CAKE

(THREE-MILK CAKE)

SONIA TURBAY

I immigrated to Canada from Colombia in 2003, with my husband and two daughters, ages eleven and fourteen. My parents and six siblings still live in Colombia. One of my sister's friends used to make this wonderful cake and I didn't want to leave Colombia without the recipe. I asked my sister to get the recipe for me but she was told that she couldn't have it because her friend's sister bakes these cakes and sells them. I guess she was afraid the recipe would become well known and her cakes would no longer sell. Still wanting to make this cake, I did some research and found something similar in Spanish. It was slightly different from what I remembered, so I experimented, baking it until it tasted exactly the way I remembered. I love this cake, but because it is so rich, I usually only make it on special occasions, or when I have guests, or when I miss my home country. Everyone loves it and asks for the recipe!

> SERVES 12

CAKE: Grease a 9 × 13 inch glass baking pan. Position the rack in the middle of the oven. Preheat the oven to 350°F.

SIFT flour and baking powder together 2 or 3 times until they are well mixed. In another bowl, beat egg whites until soft peaks form. Add sugar ¼ cup at a time, alternating with adding one egg yolk at a time. With mixer on low speed or with a spatula, alternate adding flour mixture and the ½ cup milk to egg mixture until well blended. Add vanilla. Pour batter into the greased pan and smooth out with a rubber spatula.

BAKE for about 25 to 30 minutes, or until lightly browned and a toothpick comes out clean. Place the pan on a wire rack and let cool for 10 minutes. You can leave the cake in the pan, or turn it out onto

CAKE
2 cups all-purpose flour

3 tsp baking powder

4 large eggs, separated

1 cup granulated sugar

½ cup milk

1 tsp vanilla extract

THREE-MILK MIXTURE
1 large can evaporated milk (385 mL)

1 can sweetened condensed milk (300 mL)

1 cup whipping cream

FROSTING
(CAN BE DOUBLED)
½ cup water

¾ cup granulated sugar

2 large egg whites, room temperature

½ tsp vanilla (optional)

a jelly-roll pan (not a baking sheet). With a skewer or the tines of a large meat fork, gently poke holes all over the cake "until it looks like a sieve." Be careful not to destroy the cake in the process!

THREE-MILK MIXTURE: Beat milks and cream together until they have a smooth consistency. Pour the milk mixture over the still-warm cake, spreading evenly. The milk mixture will eventually be absorbed by the cake. If you have turned the cake out onto a jelly-roll pan, the milk mixture will seep from the cake. You can spoon the milk back onto the cake until absorbed (it takes about 1 hour) or, when serving, spoon extra milk onto the plates around the slices. When all the milk has been absorbed, frost the cake.

FROSTING: Put water and sugar in a medium saucepan. Do not stir at any time. Place over medium to high heat until it begins to boil. Lower heat and continue to simmer until the syrup reaches the soft ball stage (236°F on a candy thermometer, or a drop put into a cup of very cold water will form a soft ball). Remove from heat. While the syrup is boiling, beat egg whites until they form stiff peaks. When the syrup is at the soft ball stage, pour the syrup steadily into egg whites *beating all the time* until the frosting is light and fluffy. Continue beating until the mixture cools some and thickens. Frost the cake after all the milk mixture has been absorbed. Decorate with fresh fruit or maraschino cherries. Keep in the refrigerator.

› WILD ROSE ANGEL FOOD CAKE

NANCY McLEAN

My grandmother came from Bar Harbor, Maine, and my grandparents settled in Kennebunk-port after my grandfather retired. The beach is the largest I've ever seen, anchored by two headlands of dark rocks with tidal pools. In amongst the warm saltwater pools, wild roses grow and perfume the air. Grandma made me a rose-flavoured angel food cake for my birth-day when I visited from school in Boston, and the palest pink rose-water sherbet sat beside it. I was nineteen, and at the time didn't know it would be the last time I would see her. I always have a bottle of rosewater in my cupboard, and a white wild rose is at my window.

12 large egg whites
1 cup granulated sugar
2 Tbsp rosewater
1 cup flour, sifted
1½ cups sifted icing sugar

› SERVES 10–12

PREHEAT the oven to 375°F. Use a 10-inch tube pan with removable bottom—*ungreased.*

BEAT egg whites until frothy at the highest speed of the mixer, and then very gradually add granulated sugar, beating until stiff peaks form. Add rosewater. Fold in flour and icing sugar, gently but thoroughly. Bake for 50 minutes, or until cake is browned and cracked on top.

REMOVE from the oven and invert onto a rack. Cool the cake upside down for 1 hour before turning upright. Then run a knife between the cake and the pan to loosen for ease in removal from pan. Place on a plate and cool completely before cutting with a serrated knife.

SERVE with rosewater sherbet or lemon sorbet. Close your eyes and hear the Atlantic Ocean crashing on the beach in Maine.

AUNTIE ANYA'S WALNUT CAKE

ANNE ACHESON

This recipe, originally handwritten in Russian in Auntie Anya's cookbook, came out of Russia just before the revolution in 1917. The family was in China at that time, and were never able to return to their native land. From China they went to England, Auntie Anya having married an Englishman— a friend of our family who lived in our village. Her daughter and I were like sisters and grew up together. I wrote to her quite recently to ask her for her birthday cake recipe, so here it is in Canada!

½ lb/250 g walnuts (about 2 cups)
5 large eggs, separated
½ cup + 1 Tbsp granulated sugar
1 Tbsp cornstarch
¾ cup raspberry jam

> SERVES 8

PREHEAT the oven to 350°F. Line the bottom of an 8-inch round cake pan with parchment paper.

FINELY chop walnuts in a food processor using on/off pulse. Watch carefully, as the mixture can become walnut butter before your eyes. A hand-held cheese or nut grater will grate nuts to a fluffier texture and can be used instead of a food processor.

IN a large bowl, use an electric mixer to beat egg yolks with sugar until white. Add cornstarch and mix in walnuts. In another bowl, beat egg whites until stiff. Fold about one-quarter of egg whites into the walnut mixture to lighten it, then gently fold in the remaining egg whites. Spoon batter into the prepared pan and bake for 30 minutes, then reduce the temperature to 325°F and continue baking for another 45 minutes. Cool on a rack. When cool, cut the cake in half horizontally, spread raspberry jam in the middle and place the top back on.

CHRISTMAS CHOCOLATE LOG

ANNE RIDSDALE MOTT

My grandfather, Tom Baker, had a motto: "Baker by name and baker by trade." In the bake house he built in Eastbrooke, Dinas Powys, South Wales, around 1919, he made bread for the village every day, but he delighted in making confections. Because he was also a painter and sculptor, his cakes were works of art. His loaves, in the shape of sheaves of wheat and cornucopias, were the centrepieces of the Harvest Home celebrations in the village church. He trimmed his Christmas chocolate log cakes with elves and mushrooms that he molded from marzipan. The yule log and the elves are ancient Celtic winter festival symbols. This Christmas log is light, delicious and wickedly chocolate.

> **SERVES 10**

FILLING/ICING

10 oz dark chocolate, chopped (about 1½ cups)
2 cups whipping cream
2 Tbsp rum

CAKE

4 egg yolks
2 Tbsp granulated sugar
1½ tsp vanilla extract
4 egg whites
pinch of cream of tartar
½ cup granulated sugar
¾ cup sifted cake flour
icing sugar for dusting

FILLING/ICING: Place chocolate in a large bowl. Heat cream to boiling and pour it over chocolate, stirring to melt chocolate and blend it with cream. Allow to cool at room temperature. Whip with an electric beater until fluffy and spreadable. Take one-third of the chocolate-cream mixture and add rum. Reserve the remainder of the chocolate-cream mixture for the icing.

CAKE: Preheat the oven to 375°F. Grease a 10 × 15 inch jelly-roll pan and line it with wax paper.

IN a medium bowl, beat egg yolks with the 2 tablespoons sugar until light. Beat in vanilla. In a separate large bowl that is completely clean and free from oil, beat egg whites with cream of tartar until they make soft peaks. Gradually beat in the ½ cup sugar until stiff peaks form and the mixture looks glossy. Fold half of the flour gently into the egg-yolk mixture, then fold in the other. Blend one-quarter of the egg whites into the flour-egg mixture. Fold in the rest of the egg whites.

SPREAD the batter to the edges of the prepared jelly-roll pan with a spatula and bake for 12 to 15 minutes, or until the cake begins to pull away from the sides of the pan.

TAKE the warm cake from the oven and dust it with icing sugar. Place more wax paper over the cake, cover it with a tea towel and top it with a rack. Invert the cake onto the paper, tea towel and rack, loosening it gently with a spatula. Remove the lining paper from the bottom of the cake. Roll the cake into a log (using the fresh wax paper on the outside to aid in the rolling process), starting from a short side. Wrap in a tea towel and cool on a rack.

WHEN the cake is cool, unwrap and unroll. Spread the rum-flavoured filling onto the cake. Use the wax paper again to assist in re-rolling it tightly. Cut about one-quarter off the end of the cake at an angle, so it looks like a cut log. Place the cut piece beside the main part to represent a short branch. Cover the cake with the rest of the icing and then pull a fork through the icing to represent bark. Decorate with marzipan mushrooms, elves and sprigs of holly.

TO MAKE marzipan mushrooms and elves, mold mushroom shapes and figures of elves from almond paste coloured with food colouring.

AUNTY SUE'S CHOCOLATE CAKE

AMANDA HUNT

How often do visiting children gather to guess the weight of a piece of cake? How often does a cake fall from five feet and hit the ground without losing a single crumb? How often is that cake still delicious, with the recipe much in demand? If the cake is Aunty Sue's Chocolate Cake, these events are regular occurrences. Aunty Sue's cake hails from England and has only been in the Canadian branch of the family for twenty years, but—in more ways than one—it's made quite an impact.

When my husband graduated from Rehabilitation Medicine at UBC, we celebrated by going on a four-month cycling trip to England and the Netherlands. One day in early December, we arrived sopping wet at Aunty Sue's cottage near Southampton. Aunty Sue's family did lots of ocean sailing, so she was used to bedraggled people squelching into her kitchen. She soon had our various Gortex garments festooned around the Aga; meanwhile, she was preparing for my cousin Caroline's twenty-first birthday dinner that night. Caroline's favourite dessert was her mother's chocolate cake, and every year—this special year in particular—that was the finale for the birthday feast. For two hungry travellers the cake was especially delicious, and when we left Aunty Sue's the recipe came with us. We made the cake for friends in England before we left—fabulous! Then I set out to make it again on our return to Vancouver. Something must have been lost in the translation from English ingredients to Canadian ingredients because the Canadian version of Aunty Sue's cake is extremely weighty—hence the impromptu guess-the-weight contests and falling cake near-disasters mentioned above. Nevertheless, the cake remains absolutely delicious! Must be the 1¼ pounds of sugar in the cake part and the 1¼ pounds of chocolate and 15 ounces of sour cream in the icing!

CAKE

6 oz semisweet chocolate, chopped (1 cup)

1 cup butter, room temperature

1¼ lb berry sugar (2¾ cups)

4 large eggs

1 tsp vanilla extract

8 oz all-purpose flour (1¾ cups)

1½ tsp baking powder

1¼ cup milk

ICING

20 oz/625 g semisweet chocolate chips (3 cups)

¼ tsp salt

15 oz sour cream (1¾ cups + 2 Tbsp), room temperature

CAKE: Preheat the oven to 350°F and position the racks in the centre of the oven. Spray three 8-inch round cake pans with cooking spray or grease lightly with shortening. Line the bottom of each with parchment paper.

MELT chocolate over hot (not boiling) water. Cream together butter and sugar. Beat in eggs one at a time. Add the melted chocolate and vanilla and beat again.

IN a separate bowl, sift together flour and baking powder. Fold flour and milk alternately into the creamed mixture, beginning and ending with flour.

POUR batter into 3 pans, smooth the tops and bake for about 30 to 35 minutes, or until a toothpick comes out clean. Cool in the pans on racks for 10 minutes, then remove the 3 cake layers from the pans, remove the parchment paper and finish cooling completely on the racks.

ICING: Slowly melt chocolate chips, then mix in salt and sour cream. Chill in the fridge until the mixture thickens. Watch carefully as this can happen very quickly. Spread between the layers and ice the top and sides of the cake!

> RECIPE CONVERSIONS

The following equivalents can be used to convert recipes in this book to metric measurements.

VOLUME

⅛ tsp	0.5 mL
¼ tsp	1 mL
⅓ tsp	2 mL
½ tsp	2.5 mL
¾ tsp	3.75 mL
1 tsp	5 mL
½ Tbsp	7.5 mL
1 Tbsp	15 mL
⅛ cup	25 mL
¼ cup	50 mL
⅓ cup	75 mL
½ cup	125 mL
⅔ cup	160 mL
¾ cup	180 mL
⅞ cup	200 mL
1 cup	250 mL
2 cups	500 mL
3 cups	750 mL
4 cups (1 quart)	1 litre

WEIGHT

1 oz	30 g
2 oz (⅛ lb)	60 g
3 oz	85 g
4 oz (¼ lb)	125 g
5 oz	150 g
5¼ oz	160 g
6 oz	175 g
7 oz	200 g
8 oz (½ lb)	250 g
10 oz	300 g
12 oz (¾ lb)	375 lb
14 oz	400 g
16 oz (1 lb)	500 g
2 lb	1 kg
5 lb	2.2 kg
10 lb	4.5 kg

LENGTH

⅛ inch	3 mm
¼ inch	6 mm
½ inch	13 mm
¾ inch	19 mm
1 inch	25 mm
6 inches	15 cm
8 inches	20 cm
14 inches	35 cm

COMMON CAN/PACKAGE SIZES

VOLUME

4 oz	114 mL
5½ oz	156 mL
7½ oz	213 mL
8 oz	250 mL
10 oz	284 mL
12 oz	355 mL
14 oz	398 mL
19 oz	540 mL
28 oz	796 mL

COMMON CAN/PACKAGE SIZES

WEIGHT

3¾ oz	106 g
4 oz	113 g
5 oz	142 g
6 oz	170 g
6½ oz	184 g
7¾ oz	220 g
15 oz	425 g

OVEN TEMPERATURES

145°F	63°C
150°F	65°C
160°F	71°C
165°F	74°C
175°F	79°C
200°F	95°C
250°F	120°C
300°F	150°C
325°F	160°C
350°F	175°C
375°F	190°C
400°F	205°C
425°F	220°C
450°F	230°C
475°F	240°C

BAKING PANS AND TRAYS

8-inch (square)	20 cm (2 L)
9-inch (square)	22 cm (2.5 L)
8-inch (round)	20 cm (1.2 L)
9-inch (round)	22 cm (1.5 L)
10-inch (tube pan)	25 cm (4 L)
9 × 13 inch (casserole)	22 × 33 cm (3.5 L)
10 × 15 inch (jelly-roll pan)	25 × 38 cm (2 L)
12 × 16 inch (baking sheet)	30 × 40 cm